People and Communication

Stuart Harris

Edited by George Penney with additional material by Mary Graham and Jenny Rice

PUBLISHED BY NCC PUBLICATIONS

British Library Cataloguing in Publication Data

Harris, Stuart
  People and communication.
  1. Communication
  I. Title
  302.2   P90
ISBN 0-85012-671-1

First published in 1987:

NCC Publications, The National Computing Centre Limited,
Oxford Road, Manchester M1 7ED, England.

Typeset in 10pt Times Roman by Bookworm Typesetting, Manchester;
and printed by Hobbs the Printers of Southampton.

ISBN 0-85012-671-1

Contents

Lecturer's Guide to the Course

INTRODUCTION

This course book is designed to provide students with the necessary written and oral communication skills to enable them to interpret and write documents relevant to today's business world. Parts of the course are suited to formal exposition, but the majority of the unit objectives require that students exercise their communication skills individually and in groups. Students achieve the aims of the course through an integrated approach by dividing the unit into four broad areas:

— gathering, processing and transmitting information;
— working in groups;
— information technology;
— individual research.

STAFFING

It is important that the course is not regarded as similar to a traditional English language course. While the development of self-expression and interpretative skills are valuable, the emphasis here is on group interaction, personal development and oral skills, as well as on looking at the communications process within and between firms. In particular, some role-play situations may test the communication and persuasive skills of the lecturer even more than the students, especially if some of the students happen to be lacking in confidence or motivation.

STUDENTS

The course assumes no particular age group or relevant experience, though the student should be competent in the use of the English language.

9

1 Introduction to Communication

PURPOSE OF THE SESSION

Over the course of this book we will consider the process of communication. It is a process which most people never think about analytically, a fact that is often the cause for breakdowns in communication or manipulation and abuse of the receivers. Those who do analyse the use of the communication process gain an unusual insight into human nature.

WHAT IS COMMUNICATION?

Group activity: ask the group for ideas and write them up on the blackboard.

At the centre of any definition of communication (see Figure 1.1) must be the intention of conveying a message, even if the message is abstract (modern poetry, for example). The message may not be intended for anybody in particular and may be simply for the enjoyment of the creator: so there may be no intended receiver. There will always, however, be a transmitter.

A message is usually both transmitted and received (see Figure 1.2), though some messages may not reach their destination if there is a barrier to communication. Such a barrrier may vary from a reception problem with your radio or television, to a listener whose mind is on other things or who does not understand the message.

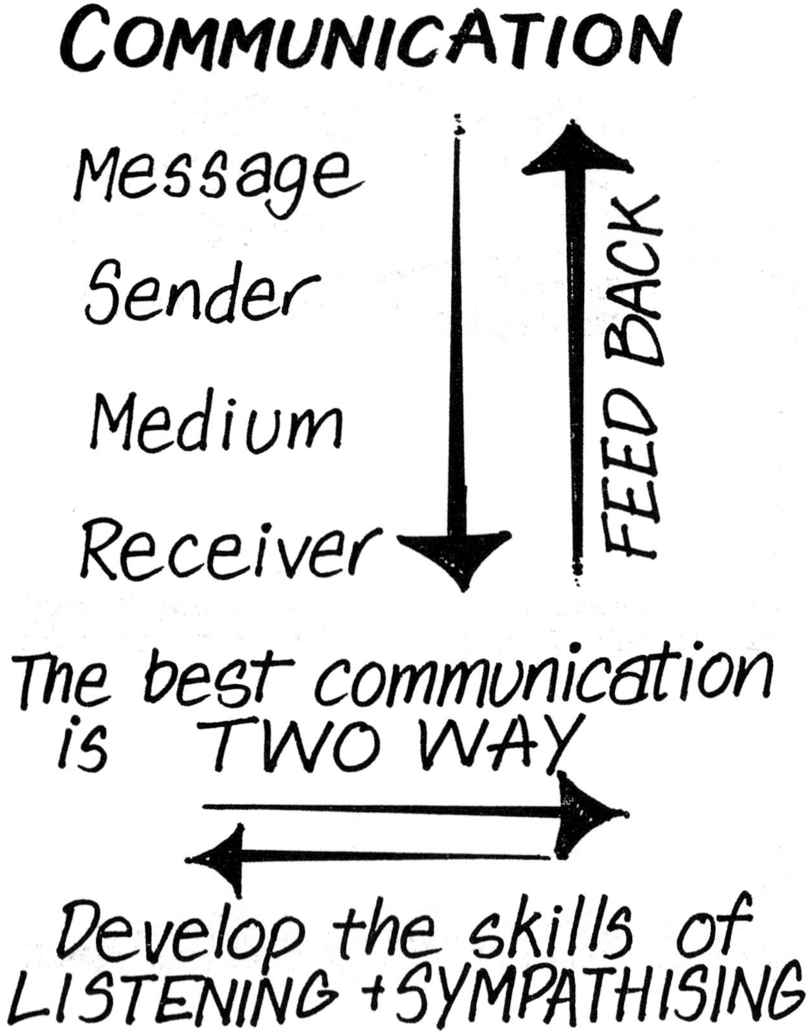

COMMUNICATION

Message

Sender

Medium

Receiver

FEED BACK

The best communication
is   TWO WAY

Develop the skills of
LISTENING + SYMPATHISING

Figure   1.1

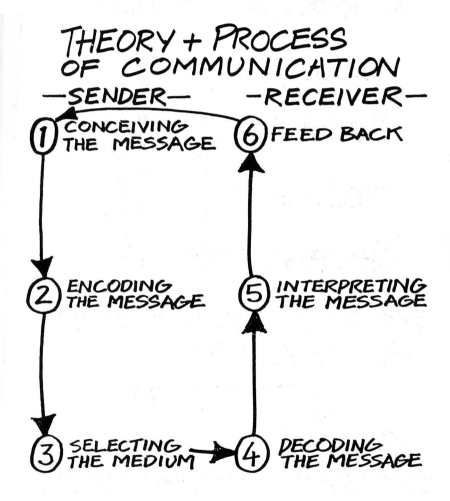

Figure   1.2

A DEMONSTRATION

Activity

(The lecturer should invite one of the group to leave the room for a few minutes. The remaining students should copy this diagram from the blackboard.)

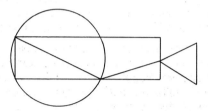

When copied, erase the diagram, cover student copies and re-capture the departed student. Instructions should then be given by the group (the lecturer hopes badly), to enable the returned student to re-draw the diagram. (Before the student re-enters the room, he/she should be requested to interpret the instructions as awkwardly as possible.) The person doing the drawing should not ask questions but should draw something absurdly wrong if, for example, no indication of size comes from the audience.

Discussion

The aim of this exercise is to show that a breakdown in the reception of a message will occur when the transmitter assumes an unreasonable amount of previous knowledge on the part of the receiver. This is a common mistake among teachers, though such examples will hopefully not be observed by the student of the present course.

One can imagine the confusion if the medium for this experiment had been the telephone. Additional problems would also have occurred if the receiver had not understood the terminology used. People working in particular environments (computer programming or engineering, for example), develop their own working terminology or restricted code to deal with specific events. The terms used may not be understood by those outside since, to the transmitter, they require an elaborated code to make understanding possible.

In all communications *we must not take the receiver's understanding for granted.*

Examples of breakdown in communication are given in the exercise on page 25.

WHAT'S SO SPECIAL ABOUT COMMUNICATION?

What is so special about communication? Animals communicate with each other, often in elaborate ways. For example, a bee discovering a plentiful supply of nectar several fields away from the hive, will return and give directions to its fellows by flying in a series of complex patterns in front of the hive. The other bees will then fly straight to the food source. Animal messages, however, tend to be limited in their purpose. (The group may care to think of the type of message that animals transmit and the lecturer to write their ideas on the blackboard.)

Although animals communicate, they do not have language. They do make noises but these tend to be situation-related: for example, a loud shriek to signify fear or pain. People also have situation-related noises (see Figure 1.3). If a Frenchman, an Englishman and a Russian were stood in line and blindfolded, you would get roughly the same noise from each of them if you stamped on their toes. The oaths that followed, however, would indicate by language the origin of the sufferer.

Jean Aitchison defines language as "a patterned system of arbitrary sound symbols, whose characteristic features of displacement, cultural transmission, productivity and duality are rare or absent in animal communication" (*Teach yourself linguistics*, 2nd ed, Fontana, 1978). Some words are perhaps less random in their component sound than others: for example the words buzz, fizz, pop and drip to some extent imitate that which they describe.

The debate on whether or not animals are capable of learning a language continues, concentrating in recent years on dolphin communications and the teaching of hand signals to apes. The miracle of human language acquisition remains a mystery. Why is it, for instance, that as infants we normally learn words and grammar at an incredible pace yet, when we have the know-how to analyse language in later years, we have such difficulty in learning enough French to buy things on holidays to France? The ability to communicate *is* special but it is often taken for granted and it is not always used to the greatest advantage (see Figure 1.4).

HOW DO WE COMMUNICATE?

We communicate in a number of ways (see Figure 1.5). Consider which medium is most appropriate (consider the example shown in Figure 1.6 and the options shown in Figure 1.7). Most of the methods illustrated employ either the use of spoken language or written symbols that represent the speech sounds. Some of the messages make no use of language at all: we call this non-verbal communication. The road sign for falling rocks, for instance, is universal: it is likely to be understood by all nationalities, as are most road signs.

OTHER INFLUENCES ON COMMUNICATION

- SITUATION CONTEXT

Role people find themselves in, eg
Stuck in lift with your boss

- FORMALITY INFORMALITY

Degree of formality
affects communication

- USE OF SPACE

Positioning of furniture, eg Being
placed on lower chair
Physical proximity

- NON VERBAL CLUES
* Facial expressions
* Gestures, hands, arms, nods
* Eye contact
* Body language

Figure 1.3

Message wrongly
conceived, vague,
ambiguous. Affected
by relationship of
sender +
receiver

Feedback not
given or wrongly
interpreted by
the sender

Message encoded
in wrong language,
tone inappropriate

Message wrongly
interpreted.
Affected by
relationship of
receiver + sender
ambiguity

Wrong medium
chosen: Offence
caused, time wasted,
expense incurred,
no written record
etc

Receiver unable
to comprehend
sender's language.
Vocab too difficult,
specialist, etc

Figure 1.4

The decision to send the message - a result of an impulse, thought process or some external stimulus

Signal passed to receiver. Nod, eye contact, written or spoken reply, etc

Appropriate language chosen - written, oral, picture or non verbal communication

Interpret the underlying meanings as well as explicit meanings in words chosen. Particularly in non verbal clues + intonation

Appropriate medium selected, eg letter or memo, phone call, meeting, interview, etc

The language used is decoded from knowledge of vocab, terms etc

Figure 1.5

CHOICE OF COMMUNICATION MEDIUM

ORG CHART

GEN MANAGER

ASST MANAGER

SUPERVISOR (YOU)

OPERATORS

You are the supervisor of a small section of 20 people. The firm you work for has been experiencing problems recently. The firm has recently lost an order from its main supplier. It is necessary for your section to be put on short-time working (3 days a week) for a short period. The other alternative is selective redundancies or even worse. It has been decided short-time working is fairest. It has been made your responsibility to inform your section.

① What communication medium would you choose?

② Why did you choose it?

Discuss the relative advantages and disadvantages of the alternative media available.

Figure   1.6

MEDIA OF COMMUNICATION

•WRITTEN

Letters, memos, minutes, reports, notes, telex, adverts press release, etc

•ORAL

Conversation, talks, speech, conferences, interviews, meetings, telephone, intercom, video, etc

•VISUAL AIDS +OTHER REINFORCING TOOLS

Dictating machine, tape recorder, graph, OHP, poster, film slide, chart, voice (intonation), face, (reinforcing non verbal clues) body language

Figure 1.7

Non-verbal communication such as the use of gestures or mannerisms is often referred to as body language. The study of this aspect of non-verbal communication (NVC) has gained in popularity, due partly to the work of Desmond Morris. We all transmit messages non-verbally. What makes NVC particularly worthy of study is that we are not usually consciously aware of the messages. The couple holding hands, on the other hand, is a communication of significance which both we and the couple are likely to consciously notice. Holding hands has acutely intense significance for the first few times a couple accept each other enough to hold hands, though it may become increasingly casual as the relationship develops. The message has clear significance to would-be suitors.

Less understood is the body language of selling, job interviews, status and authority. The salesman who is aware of the importance of eye contact is more likely to sell. An interviewing panel will be influenced by a candidate's non-verbal communication as much as by spoken responses. Consider seating in the boss's office – does the desk serve as a barrier; when seated, is the boss at a higher level than you are; are you sitting directly opposite each other; if not, who has to look sideways? – all these factors can offer the opportunity for a superior to assert his or her authority without saying a word.

In addition to the deliberate verbal communication then, a second non-verbal level operates at which we are usually less aware. This second level of communication may account for what is sometimes called 'intuition': the ability to sense, for example, that a speaker's messages are suspect. We can see therefore that there are many different methods of communication, with various advantages and disadvantages (see Figure 1.8a to 1.8c).

PEOPLE AND COMMUNICATION

Under normal circumstances, communication skills are available for us all to use. Expert communicators can use their skills to great effect, as one can witness with politicians and television presenters. Communication is also subject to abuse. A look at wartime propaganda shows how information can be transmitted in certain ways to achieve a particular effect. Even in current times, a comparison of newspaper articles covering the same news items will often reveal that some facts are being selected and interpreted for a particular purpose: perhaps to protect the ruling political power, to sensationalise scandalous aspects or to manipulate public opinion to a particular way of thinking. Analysis of newspaper reports prior to general elections is particularly fruitful.

ADVANTAGES + DISADVANTAGES
OF THE PRINCIPAL MEDIA
WRITTEN
LETTER , MEMOS, REPORTS ETC

ADVANTAGES Provides written record
evidence of despatch + receipt.
Can relay complex ideas, provides
analysis, evaluation, summary. Can
be duplicated. Can confirm, interpret,
clarify oral communication.

DISADVANTAGES Takes time, can be
expensive, more formal +
distant. Can cause problems of
interpretation, instant feedback
impossible, difficult to modify message
once sent. Exchange of views, attitudes
only possible over period of time.

Figure   1.8a

ORAL COMMUNICATION
FACE TO FACE, INTERVIEWS, MEETINGS, ETC

ADVANTAGES Direct medium, advantage of physical proximity + usually sight and sound of receiver /sender, instant interchange of opinions etc. Instant feedback, easier to convince, persuade, contribution/participation of all present.

DISADVANTAGES More difficult to hold ground in face of opposition. More difficult to control if number of people take part. Lack of time to think things out. Quality of decision-making may be inferior. Often no written record + sometimes disputes result.

Figure 1.8b

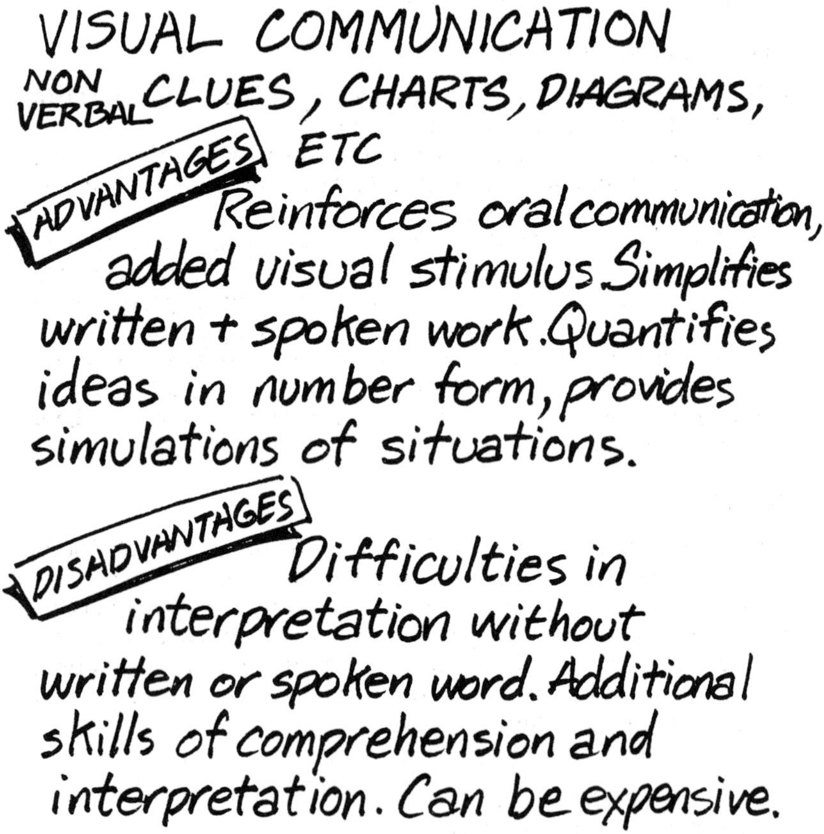

VISUAL COMMUNICATION

NON VERBAL CLUES, CHARTS, DIAGRAMS, ETC

ADVANTAGES Reinforces oral communication, added visual stimulus. Simplifies written + spoken work. Quantifies ideas in number form, provides simulations of situations.

DISADVANTAGES Difficulties in interpretation without written or spoken word. Additional skills of comprehension and interpretation. Can be expensive.

Figure   1.8c

Hopefully the link between people and communication is now becoming apparent. It is not only the item of information or message that influences people, but the way in which the transmitter chooses to broadcast the message: from the selection of words to the way that they are presented. This course book recognises this link and aims not only to develop your communication skills but also to make you more aware of the communication process and its effect on others.

Summary of Course Objectives

— To increase the student's effectiveness in work situations, through the development of language and social skills;
— to contribute to the student's personal development by fostering the ability to communicate with and relate to others as individuals, in groups and within organisations;
— to develop the student's skills in dealing with information in various forms, so that he/she is better able to acquire, evaluate and organise it for his/her own purposes, and to present it in effective form when required, in study and in employment;
— to encourage in the student a sensitivity to the ideas and attitudes of others, an awareness of how these can be affected by the student and other people, and a preparedness to adapt to them where necessary.

ACTIVITY

As a group activity either arrange for somebody to 'accidentally' walk into the room mid-session, or ask a member of the group to leave the room for 15 minutes. The group must now try collectively to produce a written description of the missing person: height, weight, colour of eyes, hair colour and style, clothes, personal effects, etc. When finished, invite the person back into the room and compare your written description with the 'real thing'.

EXERCISE 1

A Conceiving a Message Wrongly

A passenger is travelling by coach from Birmingham to Manchester. The Manchester coach leaves bay 9 at 10.55. It is 10.55 and a coach is standing at bay 9. The passenger dashes to that bay and asks "Is this bay 9?". Another passenger answers "yes". Passenger catches the coach as it leaves the coach station. It is the wrong coach. It is the one for Scotland which is late and also leaves from bay 9.

Explain what has gone wrong and where the breakdown fits into the 'circle' describing communication theory. (Include the second passenger's response.)

B   Ways of Interpreting Messages

1   How many ways could the message shown in Figure 1.9 be interpreted by the junior?

2   Point out all the influences which could affect these interpretations.

Figure   1.9

TECHNIQUES FOR IMPROVED COMMUNICATION

Feedback

An engineering term, 'feedback' refers to the ability of certain complex machines to check on their own performance and correct it if necessary. This principle is of prime importance in human communication. We must constantly be alert for clues to whether or not we are being understood (facial expression, head nods, etc).

The importance of feedback is illustrated by a simple exercise. Two students are seated back-to-back with a table in front of each of them. Identical sets of children's building blocks are placed on the tables. One of the students proceeds to build any structure he chooses, using all the blocks, and at the same time instructs the other student to build an identical structure. The receiver is forbidden to respond in any way. The absence of feedback makes the task, in most cases, impossible, as false perceptions creep in and minor errors go uncorrected and become magnified. Additionally, the exercise makes the point that communication gains in speed as more and more feedback is permitted.

Using a Number of Communication Channels

Observation

In a face-to-face situation we can observe the other person and judge his responses by his 'total behavioural set', ie changes of facial expression and more subtle body movements that communicate anger, disbelief, impatience, etc. Tone of voice is equally informative, for example as a measurement of enthusiasm.

Listening with the 'Third Ear'

There is a hidden content in most communication which can only be inferred by the listener (latent content, versus manifest content). The listener should try to go beyond the logical verbal meaning where there is evidence that emotional feeling is involved, bearing in mind the need to keep imagination in check.

Speaking Patterns

It is important to be aware of the difference in speaking patterns. Some people speak with drawn-out pauses between thoughts or sentences, and if they are interrupted they fail to reveal all their original ideas. Failure to adjust and to synchronise to the speech patterns of others, as well as causing ideas to be lost, can result in long silent periods which cause discomfort.

The Merits of Face-to-face Communication

— Ease, through frequency of use of voice rather than written medium;
— immediacy of feedback;
— more credibility given to what we hear someone say rather than to words attributed to them in print.

However, it is important to note that written communication allows both for more permanency and for easier assimilation of complex material. In the case of the need to communicate with a larger number of people, written communication is also administratively more convenient.

Sensitivity to the World of the Receiver

We need to predict the impact of what we say and do, tailoring our message to fit the receiver's vocabulary, emotional state, interests and values; in short we need to empathise.

Awareness of Symbolic Meaning

We must try and be aware of the symbolic meaning of what we say and write and be prepared to revise our statements if they evoke unfavourable reactions, however irrational they may appear to us.

The Timing of Messages

Consider the following example: Management announces that a foreman, Green, is to retire and will be replaced in a few months by Williams, at present employed in another department. One of the employees spreads a rumour that Williams is a tyrant who favours 'crawlers'. Before Williams takes up the new post, a petition is sent to Management asking for a different foreman to be assigned. When Williams finally takes up his new post, everything he says and does is fitted to the picture already built up; even harmless statements are interpreted as threats and every action scrutinised for favouritism! What lessons are to be learned from this situation?

Introducing Redundancy

When giving a direct order or transmitting technical information we should make sure that the message includes a certain element of redundancy. Then, if any word or phrase is misunderstood, there will be other elements of the message which will carry the point. Familiarity can also lead to communication breakdown; we tend to ignore many of the messages which we receive simply because they sound so familiar. The problem, in short, is to balance the need for redundancy to support words and phrases of crucial importance and the need to achieve a pattern which has originality and avoids repetition of cliches.

This techniques section can be summed up as:

$$
\text{Efforts to Communicate}
\left\{
\begin{array}{l}
\text{Feedback} \\
\text{Many Channels} \\
\text{Face-to-face Communication} \\
\text{Sensitivity to Receiver} \\
\text{Symbolic Meanings} \\
\text{Timing of Messages} \\
\text{Redundancy}
\end{array}
\right\}
\text{Clear Message}
$$

A REMINDER: USING THE COMMUNICATION PROCESS EFFECTIVELY

As Sender

— When composing a message decide what actions or response you want;
— choose the language or combination of written/spoken/non-verbal communication most suitable for the type of communication;
— take time to structure your ideas logically;
— select the medium which is most likely to achieve your aim;
— put yourself in the receiver's position. Will he/she understand the words chosen? What is the context? What seems to be his/her emotional state?;
— take care that the message cannot be misinterpreted. Avoid being vague or ambiguous;
— check for feedback. Decide if you need an answer. Look for an indication of attitude.

As Receiver

— Give the message your whole attention;
— check that the medium suits your needs; tactfully give help if this is inappropriate;
— ensure full *comprehension*. Check references and ask for explanations if necessary;
— check that *you* are interpreting correctly. Is there an underlying meaning or implication? Check 'how' the message comes across – ie the manner in which it is communicated;
— ensure that you supply sufficient and appropriate feedback.

EXERCISE 2 – IN-TRAY ASSIGNMENT

You are the office clerk in a small company. As there are few office staff you have a variety of duties to perform. As well as general office tasks, you are responsible for opening the mail in the morning and forwarding it to its correct department. It is Monday morning and you find the items that follow (Figures 1.10 to 1.17) in your 'in tray'. It is your task to deal with them as efficiently as possible; to help you do this, follow the procedure given below:

— arrange them in order of priority;
— state what action you would take for each one;
— complete any written form of communication necessary.

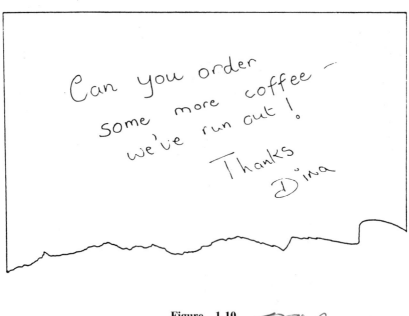

Figure   1.10

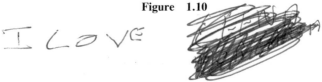

VISION GRAPHICS

MEMORANDUM

Date: 2.3.87.

Reference: TJ/RA

To: Miss Lewis

From: Transport Dept.

Subject:

Ring Eastleigh 2231 to book Mr. Richards, car for a 12,000 mile service, today if possible.

Figure 1.11

MESSAGE FORM

Time of Call ..... 5 p.m. .... Date. 27-2-87

Name of Caller .. Sue Lewis ....

Name and Address of Firm

....

....

....

Tel. No. 456544 .... Ext. No. ....

Receiver of Call .... Jenny Lewis ....

MESSAGE ⊢————

Your sister, Sue, phoned late
Friday afternoon. She has no idea
what to buy your parents for their
silver wedding anniversary. Have you
any suggestions?
         Can you ring her when you
have a spare moment?

Taken By. Sara Jones ....

Figure   1.12

VISION GRAPHICS

MEMORANDUM

To: All Staff
From: Secretary of Staff Club
Subject:

Date:27.2.07.
Reference:

We must know how many staff want to come on the trip to London on Saturday next as soon as possible. It may otherwise have to be cancelled.

Figure   1.13

12 Oak Road,
Kings Park,
Hoxley. HK 29 4QP

27-2-87

The Personnel Manager,

Vision Graphics,

2 Low Street,

Hoxley HH 19 4Q, z

Dear Sir or Madam,

My father used to work for your company until he retired two years ago. I have recently been made redundant by Jones and Co. Ltd. I am a skilled printer and would welcome the opportunity to work for you, if there should happen to be any vacancies.

Yours faithfully,

Paul Green.

Figure 1.14

VISION GRAPHICS

MEMORANDUM

To: Miss Lewis
From: Peter Richards, Manager.
Subject: Taxi

Date: 2.3.87.
Reference: SH/PR.

Please order me a taxi for 9.30 a.m. to take me to a
meeting at Thoms and Sons Ltd., High Street.

Figure 1.15

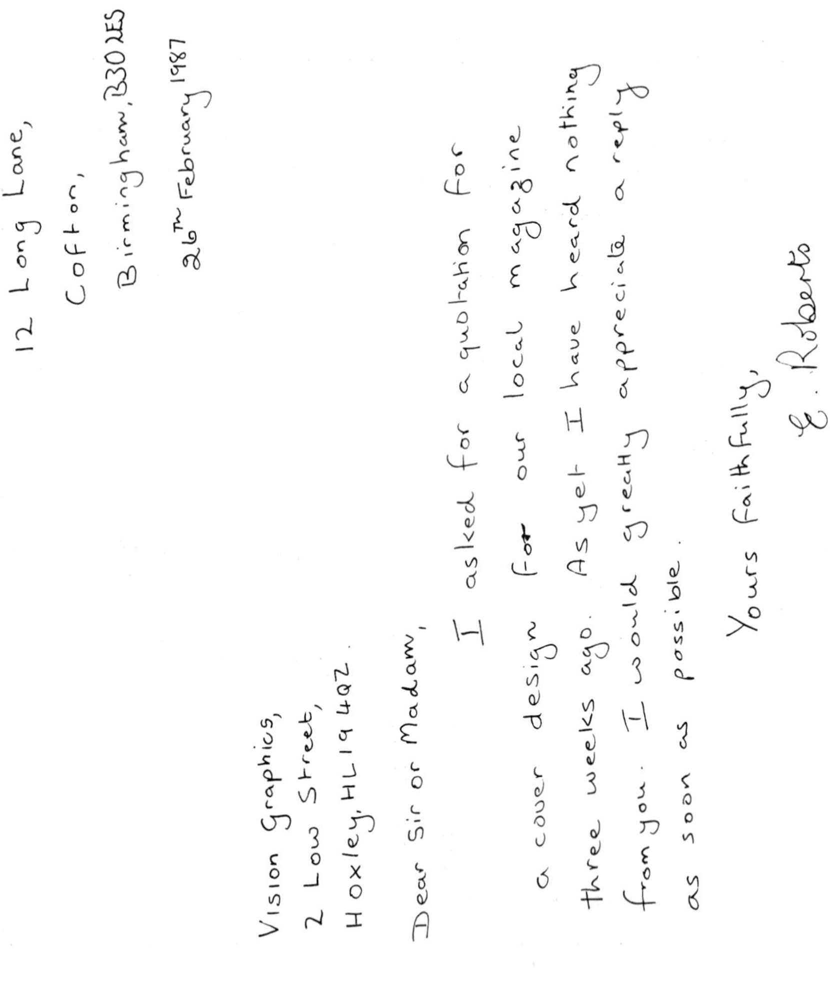

12 Long Lane,
Cofton,
Birmingham, B30 2ES
26th February 1987

Vision Graphics,
2 Low Street,
Hoxley, HL19 4QZ.

Dear Sir or Madam,

I asked for a quotation for a cover design for our local magazine three weeks ago. As yet I have heard nothing from you. I would greatly appreciate a reply as soon as possible.

Yours faithfully,

E. Roberts

Figure 1.16

┌───┐
│ ─│MESSAGE FORM│─────────────────────────────── │
│   │
│ Time of Call ......9 a·m.............. Date..2-3-87. │
│ Name of Caller .....Tony Lyons - Sales Manager... │
│ Name and Address of Firm   │
│ -- --- -- -- -- -- -- -- -- -- -- -- -- -- -- -- - │
│ -- --- -- -- -- -- -- -- -- -- -- -- -- -- -- -- - │
│ -- --- -- -- -- -- -- -- -- -- -- -- -- -- -- -- - │
│ Tel. No.............. Ext. No..35.......   │
│ Receiver of Call......Jenny Lewis................. │
│   │
│ MESSAGE ├───   │
│   │
│   Can you book a 1st Class   │
│   seat on a train to London tomorrow   │
│   morning at about 9·am for Tony.   │
│   Let him know the departure   │
│   time as soon as possible.   │
│   │
│   │
│ Taken By....Sara Jones............   │
└───┘

Figure   1.17

2   Study Skills

IMPROVING YOUR READING

Reading is a skill we all take very much for granted. It has probably not occurred to you that you can teach yourself to read BETTER and FASTER. This chapter aims to start you in this direction. By the time you have worked through the exercises you should be a better and faster reader than you were before.

How to Read Better

One very useful approach to studying any written material (a handout, especially if it is a long one, a book or an article), is known as SQ3R (Survey, Question, Read, Recall, Review). The five steps (see Figure 2.1) in this approach are:

— SURVEY the material first, to get some idea of what parts (if any) you will need to study in detail. To help you in this task, scan the table of contents; if the book has a full description of the contents of chapters this is often a useful guide. The Preface or Introduction may also be useful in helping you find out quickly what the book is about. If a particular chapter looks of interest note it but don't read it yet. First look to see if there is a summary – perhaps at the end; check headings to sections and any emphasised sections.

— Think up QUESTIONS that will give purpose to your study and allow you to read with anticipation (eg 'Why does the author divide up his material in this way?', 'What are the main themes: are these useful to me?').

— READ the material (preferably two or three times quite fast rather than once slowly).

— Stop after each section of material to RECALL what you have read and make brief notes of the main ideas and important details. Is the section of key importance to you?

— REVIEW what you have read (to test the accuracy of your notes) by quickly running through the four previous steps again.

HOW TO READ BETTER

- Survey
- Questions
- Read
- Recall
- Review

(SQ3R)

Figure 2.1

During the 'Read' stage of SQ3R:

— pick out the main idea in each paragraph – often this will be contained in the first or last sentence;

— look for important details, eg proofs, examples, supports for main idea;

— study the author's diagrams and illustrations – they may make clear what the text does not;

— be sceptical. Don't take the author's word on trust; look for him to justify every statement he makes. (If he doesn't and the point is an important one, check with another book or fellow student and later with your lecturer);

— don't be afraid to skip paragraphs and whole sections if you can see that they are not relevant to your purpose. There's no law that says you've got to read every page of a book;

— if, after chewing over a particular section for some time, you still find it difficult to understand, take a break. Try to discuss the difficulty with other students or with a lecturer or find another author's treatment of the topic; then come back and read the passage again – two or three times if necessary.

How to Read Faster

Being able to read faster (see Figure 2.2) will enable you to use the ideas on how to read better (above), to get the best possible overall results. Most students spend a great deal of time working on books and other printed materials. They would be able to use this time more effectively if they could read faster. And the truth is that most people could read at least as fast again as their normal speed, and still understand just as well. Slow readers tend to read one word at a time, often mouthing the words as they do so, and to take frequent glances back at words they have already seen. Some read so slowly that by the time they have got to the end of a paragraph, or even a sentence, they may have forgotten how it began. Here are five ways you can start helping yourself to read faster:

— have your eyes tested – many people turn out to need reading glasses for continuous study;

— make sure you don't mouth words or say them aloud as you read;

— try to take in 'thought-units' (two or three words at a time) so that your eye stops only three or four times in a line of print instead of at every word;

— practise reading faster (force yourself):
  • time your reading of magazine articles of known length – and test recall of the contents;

HOW TO READ FASTER

- Check vision
- Don't mouth words
- Thought units – not words
- Practise
- Vary speed to complexity

- Read widely
- Use dictionary
- List words relevant to your subject

Figure   2.2

- read all your study material faster, even if you have to read it more than once.

The aim of the above exercises is to be able to vary your reading speed according to the complexity of the material and the purpose for which you are reading it. If you are simply trying to get the overall gist of a piece of narrative, you should be able to read two or three times as fast as when you are trying to unravel the detailed development of a complex argument. But even when the material is particularly difficult, you may benefit from scanning it through quickly first before you get down to reading it more intensively. Don't expect every piece of text you look at to yield its full meaning immediately.

Build up your vocabulary by the following methods:

— read widely;
— use a dictionary whenever new words crop up in your reading; note new words;
— make a list of the meanings of words commonly used in your subjects; this vocabulary-broadening activity should be separate from your practice at reading faster.

Now read the passage given in Exercise 1, shown on page 48. Carefully note the time, in minutes and seconds, at which you start reading and the time at which you finish. In this task, which we will call 'search reading', you are searching for certain key words or phrases which help you locate specific information. Words which are not closely related to what you are looking for need no more than a passing glance. An even simpler task than 'search reading' is 'scanning' in which you scan a passage as rapidly as possible in order to find a single fact such as the figure for Brazil's lowest trade surplus since 1983.

Skimming

So far we have looked at what might be called 'receptive reading', where you have little clear purpose beyond needing to obtain a good general understanding, and at 'search reading' and 'scanning', where your purpose is very clear. A question which remains is : how do you decide on your purpose until you have found out what an author has to say?

For this, and for other reasons, 'skimming' (see Figure 2.3) is a very useful skill. Skimming involves going rapidly through a text while making certain judgements, and remembering only certain things. It may be used:

— to decide, by previewing a text, whether to read it in total and if so why to read it (ie for what purpose);

SKIMMING

- Preview

- Search

- Gist

- Revision

Figure   2.3

— to decide how to read it (eg whether to read carefully making
  detailed notes, or merely to use it for search reading in order to
  gain information on a certain topic);
— to read it to obtain a rough idea of what the writer has to say (ie
  for the gist of his meaning);
— to review something you have already read, for revision for an
  examination or to refresh your memory for some other purpose.

The important common factor in all these uses of skimming is that
they involve selectivity on the part of the reader. Skimming is also
always done quickly: at a speed at least two and a half to three times that
which you would use to read the passage if you were using receptive
reading rather than skimming. One other use of skimming is, strange as
it may seem, in tackling very difficult texts. It will sometimes be better
to read text through quickly two or three times, without attempting full
understanding of the more baffling points, until they become gradually
clearer.

MAKING NOTES

Notes provide a brief written record of larger pieces of work, eg an
article, a chapter in a book, a talk or a television programme. Making
notes keeps your mind active as you read. It makes you think and
concentrate – so you learn and remember better. Don't forget,
however, that there may be alternatives to note-taking you may wish to
use, eg underlining in a book.

The important things to remember in note-taking are:

— the main ideas and themes must be clear;
— avoid detail and repetition;
— your notes must mean something to *you* so wherever possible *use
  you own words*;
— use a system which works for you.

How to Make Notes

Linear Note-making

This is the traditional type of note-making which most of us are familiar
with. Headings and sub-headings are used, with lettering, numbering
and indentations used for sections and sub-sections. You will see that
parts of this book are set out in this way.

Although you are probably already familiar with this form of noting,
try Exercises 2 and 3 given on pages 49 and 50. You will find that linear
notes can be useful for summarising existing information but may not be

so useful for such things as trying to recall previously learned material or even generating new ideas round a topic.

Patterned Note-making

Traditional linear notes look very neat but may not show adequately the relationships between the ideas and themes in the subject you are noting. You may therefore find that you need to approach note-making from a different angle. A useful alternative to linear notes is patterned notes which link together key ideas/concepts. The basic unit is a 'spray' of ideas, as shown in Figure 2.4.

Uses for patterned notes:

— for recalling things or for generating new ideas;
— for making your own notes from written or spoken material.

Tips for patterns:

— use only KEY WORDS – don't waste time on unnecessary words;
— all words should be PRINTED for ease of reading;
— arrange the printed words ON the LINES which link up the various parts of the pattern.

When you are using patterns for recall or creativity let your mind go free. You will be surprised at the speed with which you generate ideas.

Exercise in Patterned Note-making

Without pausing for further thought write down as much information as you can in the form of KEY WORDS on LINES to form a pattern around a particular topic, eg the basic economic decisions which firms have to make in order to survive in the commercial world.

Problems

The difficulties you may have experienced are most likely to have been:

— organisation and order;
— sequence of ideas;
— importance of some ideas;
— beginning and ending.

Solutions

If you are using patterns for note-making from a book or lecture, it may be a good idea to use two pages of notes concurrently or to use an A4 page on its side, using one side for patterns, the other for linear detail or diagrams, etc.

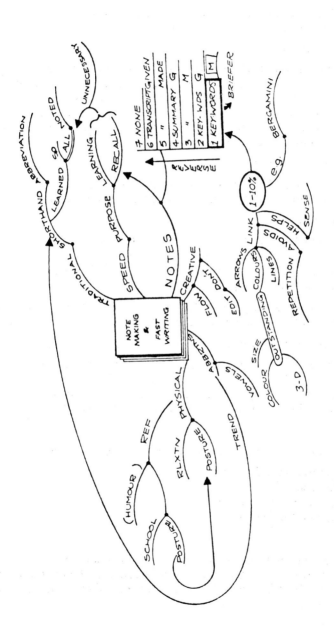

Figure 2.4

EXERCISE 1

Read the passage in Figure 2.5 and answer the question: why is Brazil finding it difficult to repay its external debt?

Note the time you start and finish in minutes and seconds.

Fears rise over Brazil debts

Fears rise over Brazil debts

BY IVO DAWNAY AND ALEXANDER NICOLL

CONCERN WAS mounting last night that the fall in Brazil's foreign trade surplus would shortly force it to delay repayments on its $109bn (£71.43bn) external debt.

There was no official confirmation of rumours that the Brazilian Government was about to suspend payments, but foreign bankers are conscious of the gravity of the situation. They expect a delay of some kind, though not necessarily an official moratorium.

The severity of Brazil's crisis was underlined by Mr Paul Volcker, chairman of the US Federal Reserve Board, who told a congressional committee that the country was in a "grave economic crisis."

The Fed chairman also issued an urgent warning about the outlook for the Third World debt problems.

Describing the strategy for tackling the debt problem, the so-called "Baker plan" was "bogged down" by the failure of complete bank financings for a number of heavily indebted nations. Mr Volcker said: "This is threatening the whole process."

Mr Volcker said confidence had been lost in Brazil. In spite of firm, constructive steps that had made the economy competitive for a while, high inflation had returned and the trade position had deteriorated. These factors could make it difficult to raise money from commercial banks.

Brazil's ambassador to the US, Mr Marcílio Marques Moreira, was reported to have returned to Washington after consultations with President Jose Sarney and other top officials. He was expected to spell out to the US the seriousness of Brazil's shortage of funds.

One Brazilian official quoted by Reuters said: "We are going to have to warn creditors that we cannot pay more than we can afford."

Rumours of a debt move and of impending economic measures pushed the dollar sharply higher on Brazil's illegal black market. It rose as high as Cr 30 compared with official rates of about Cr 18.5. Gold prices also rose 10 per cent above the New York market price.

Foreign bankers believe a delay in payments could take the form of a centralisation of exchange controls, and that it would be accompanied by assurances that Brazil was taking the step out of necessity and not in defiance of its creditors.

Another option being mooted is a formal suspension of some repayments for a short period, perhaps three months. This would give Brazil a breathing space while it negotiated fresh arrangements with creditors.

The recent sharp deterioration in Brazil's payments position is expected to heighten pressure on the Government to relax its steadfast refusal to adopt a programme of economic adjustment under the auspices of the International Monetary Fund.

Brazil was counting on at least a $1bn monthly trade surplus to meet its payments, but in January the surplus was the lowest since 1983, dropping to a mere $129m from $701m a year ago.

Brazil's trade surplus began its downward fall last October, when it dropped to $210m. Since 1984, it had been averaging more than $1bn a month – enough to meet the interest payments.

Figure   2.5   Extract from *The Financial Times*, 20 February 1987

EXERCISE 2

Rewrite in linear narrative form the weather conditions in this area of the West Midlands for 'today' through until 'tomorrow afternoon' (Figure 2.6). Make a comparison between these temperatures and those in Europe over the same period.

	This Evening	Tonight	Tomorrow morning	Tomorrow afternoon
Weather	Dry	Dry	Dry	Dry
State of sky	Bright	Broken	Bright	Bright
Temperature	15C(59F)	10C(45F)	13C(59F)	15C(59F)
Wind	Light SSW	Light S	Mod S	Mod SW
Remarks	Isolated showers possible.			

Outlook for the following day: Dry, sunny spells.

Weather Mail

SUN AND MOON

Sun rises 6.02, sets 8.10. Moon rises 1.14 am, sets 7.52 am.

WEATHER ABROAD

Algiers: s. 20C(68F); Amsterdam: s. 15C(59F); Athens: c. 17C(63F); Barcelona: s. 17C(63F); Berlin: s. 13C(55F); Brussels: s. 18C(64F); Copenhagen: c. 9C(48F); Dublin: s. 13C(55F); Florence: s. 19C(66F); Geneva: s. 17C(63F); Innsbruck: s. 18C(64F); Lisbon: c. 19C(66F); Majorca: s. 18C(64F); Malta: s. 17C(63F); Nice: s. 16C(61F); Oslo: f. 13C(55F); Paris: s. 21C(70F); Stockholm: f. 9C(48F); Vienna: f. 15C(59F).

Key: s. sunny; c. cloudy; f. fair.

YOUR £ ABROAD

This is what holidaymakers can expect to receive for their pound in overseas currencies:

	Today	Y'day
French franc	9.68	9.65
Deutschmark	2.90	2.90
Peseta	203	202
Lira	2,070	2,050
Aust schilling	20.35	20.30
US dollar	1.62	1.62
Greek drachma	210	210
Yugoslav dinar	940	935

Warmest place in Britain yesterday: Jersey, 23C(73F); **coldest:** Tummel Bridge (Tayside), -3C(27F); **wettest:** Lerwick (Shetland), 0.01 ins; **sunniest:** Leuchars (East Scotland), 13.0 hrs.

Birmingham Airport Met Office readings for the 24 hours to 0900 hours today:-

Maximum temperature: 20.7C (69.3F).

Night minimum temperature: 6.8C(44.2F).

Sunshine: 11.2 hours.

Rainfall: Nil.

Humidity: 0600 hours 97%, 1200 hours 64%, 1800 hours 49%.

Barometer: corrected to sea level (0900 hrs), 1020.7 mb (30.14 ins).

Wind: SE. 8 mph.

Sea passages: Channel, North Sea: Slight.
Irish Sea: Moderate.

Figure 2.6 Extract from the *Birmingham Evening Mail*

EXERCISE 3

Reproduce the substance of the article below: "Somalia famine as rains fail" (Figure 2.7), in note form, using not more than 125 words in all (the original is around 400 words in length). It is not necessary to avoid the wording of the original but you will obviously earn credit for the intelligent selection of material and the logical arrangement of your notes.

Somalia famine as rains fail

From Shyama Perera in Mogadishu

THE Somali Government is to declare a drought emergency after the failure of the spring rains for the second year in succession. Up to two million people could be affected.

Nomads living in the central region of the country have reported many cattle dead or dying, and there has been an influx of displaced persons and livestock to neighbouring towns.

About 54 people, mainly children, are known to have died already from drought-related diseases, but it is thought the real figure is over 300. The Ministry of the Interior said yesterday that if the rains had not come by the end of this week, they would declare the central region an emergency area. This would allow donors to release reserve funds to finance food and water stocks.

Surrounding areas, such as the river town of Giohar, have had some rain, and water levels are high. But there is little or no grazing and the survival rate of nomadic livestock in the area is low because they are often too weak to move and fall victim to sleeping sickness carried by the tsetse fly.

Conditions around the central region of Galgadud are said to be critical. Mr Cabdi Arden Noor, permanent secretary at the Ministry of the Interior, said adequate water supplies were being trucked to the worst areas and Oxfam had installed hand-pumps at bore holes for nomads who could not afford trucked supplies. However, these are only stalling tactics and in one of the hardest hit areas, Dusa Mareb, food supplies ran out 20 days ago.

The roads are already strewn with the carcases of dead animals and the air is filled with the stench of rotting flesh. In Somalia, with its 65 per cent nomadic population, livestock is the equivalent of currency.

Oxfam's Somalia director, Mr Steve Cavell, said yesterday that upwards of 100,000 people could be left destitute through loss of livestock.

Even if the rains break through in the next week, it will do little to ease the situation and will cause widespread disease among those with weakened resistance as a result of malnutrition and dehydration.

Nomad migration patterns throughout the country indicate this crisis could be worse than the crippling drought of 1975.

Figure 2.7   Excerpt from *The Guardian*, 23 February 1987

ASSIGNMENT 1

Using Library and Reference Sources

Catalogues

Look up the following in the Author Catalogue:

— the titles of two books by a writer whose surname begins with A;
— the name of two publications issued by the Ministry of Education;
— write down the names of published books by J D Salinger;

Look up the following in the Subject Catalogue:

— the titles of two books with the classification numbers of 001.64 and 301.42;
— the classification number of the subject Japanese Cookery.

Periodicals

Find out which periodicals relevant to Business Studies are taken by the library.

Information Sources

List the information sources provided by the Quick Reference Section of your Central Library.

List the titles of reference material which would be useful to a large exporting company.

General Information

Provide answers to the following questions and list the source of your information. If possible provide more than one information source:

— How many companies is   director of?
— How many companies are subsidiaries of   ?
— Locate a suitable hotel in your nearest city for an overnight stay for a business man requiring conference facilities.
— The rate of exchange of the £ at 2.00 pm today.
— The currency of Greece and its rate of exchange in £ sterling and US dollars.
— Times of flights to New York arriving before 5.30 pm local time (Mon to Fri).

Reference Books

Provide answers to the following questions and name your reference source:

— Can you fly from Tunis airport to Bombay?
— Who or what is COSIRA?
— Who is chairman of   ?
— How many companies does   own?
— What does the firm   manufacture?
— What is the European Development Fund?
— How many years service do female employees have to accumulate to be eligible for maternity leave and pay?
— What categories of tax do companies pay on their profits?
— What was the national value of exports in 1980?
— What is the parent company of   ?
— What is the current bank rate?
— Give the name and address of a company that manufactures protective clothing.
— What law governs fire safety in work places?
— What was the total in £ sterling of French imports to the UK in 1980?
— What was the gross profit of the UK vehicles industry in 1978?
— Give the name and address of a company that sells vending machines.
— What is the Registered Office address of   ?
— Which road do you take from   to   ?
— What was the total national number of unemployed in 1981?
— Which company owns   ?
— Who is your MP? (give the name of your constituency).
— What is the capital of Yugoslavia and name its government leaders?

3 Written Communication

INTRODUCTION

In business, the first impact one person makes on others is often through words on paper – in the form of a letter, report, memo, or advertisement. This means that in many instances the first – and perhaps the only – opportunity one has to influence others is by one's skill at putting one's thoughts on paper. The most common forms of written communication that one is likely to come across in business are the letter and the office memo. In the day-to-day running of an office it is often essential to inform staff promptly of important facts or instructions. Often a telephone message saves time but the sender cannot be sure that the message will be retained accurately. A written memorandum, in this case, is the most suitable form of communication. However, as this is an open form of correspondence, no confidential information should be included; see Figure 3.1.

VISION GRAPHICS

MEMORANDUM

To: Date:
From: Reference:
Subject:

Figure 3.1

Since letters are the most common form of written communication, we shall concentrate at this stage on letter-writing. The same principles, however, apply to all forms of written communication. These principles are concerned with: purpose, content, structure, style and layout (see Figure 3.2).

PURPOSE

Communications generally, and letters in particular, may have three purposes, either separately or in combination: to inform; to instruct; to influence. We can examine each of them in turn:

To Inform

A letter simply giving information will usually be in response to a request for such, or may be a confirmation of information already provided in another way. Whether the information being given is new to the recipient or is confirmation of information already given, it is in the interests of both sender and receiver that the information is given in as few words as possible (without at the same time giving offence or alarm). Traditional business jargon such as 'your valued communication of 6th ult' or 'may we respectfully draw your attention to' do no more than give the impression that the sender is old fashioned – and old; see Figure 3.3.

Of course not all letters can be as short as these examples. Some matters require delicate handling: a complaint, for instance, about an item of merchandise, or the behaviour of a member of one's family. Even then, there is no excuse for filling a piece of business stationery with meaningless words; this is liable to make the recipient even more cross than before.

To Instruct

A letter can do many things: give delivery instructions for goods, call someone up into the army, and so on. The only important things here are clarity and precision. The main content is usually standard, often pre-printed. We are not especially concerned here with this kind of communication.

To Influence

The most important person *you* need to influence is a potential employer, and we shall return later to the question of letters of application. The purpose of this kind of letter would be to influence the recipient to grant you an interview. Can you think of some other

WRITTEN COMMUNICATION PRINCIPLES

PURPOSE:
to inform, instruct, influence
CONTENT:
determined by purpose
STRUCTURE:
aid to logical thought
STYLE/VOCABULARY:
suited to reader
LAYOUT/APPEARANCE:
crisp + clean, reflecting
structure

Figure 3.2

BREVITY

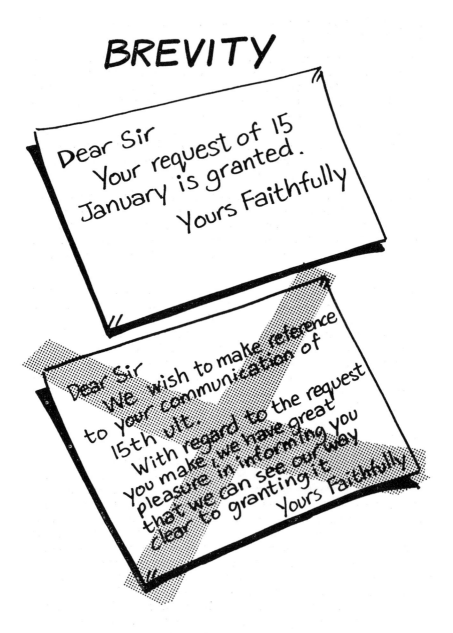

Figure   3.3

examples of letters where the purpose is to influence people? – you will find further examples in Figure 3.4.

In order to influence someone, you have to convince them that you had them specifically in mind when you were writing the letter. So a sales letter distributed generally throughout the population will not be very effective if it includes the words: "if you are over 40", or "this offer applies to all males under 55". The necessary preliminary research should have been done to exclude those outside the target age-group or other category from the circulation list. Otherwise the mail-out will be unnecessarily expensive and will annoy some recipients who might be potential customers for another product or service from the firm.

Many organisations use their computers to produce letters which appear to be personally addressed, often, for instance, scattering the recipient's name at various points in the letter or accompanying literature. This probably influences some recipients positively – just so long as the letter does not begin, "Dear Mr Smith, If you are over 40 . . .".

Look at the examples given in Figure 3.5. If you are trying to influence someone, whether to use your product, or to withdraw a complaint they have made, which would be the best way of beginning your first sentence? Can you suggest other better ways? Different people need different treatment of course, but if you do not know your recipient, express your meaning completely and clearly, while paying them the compliment of assuming that they are intelligent and well-informed, without making unwarranted assumptions about their level of knowledge.

CONTENT

The content depends, of course, on the subject-matter, but it also depends on the level of knowledge and level of need on the part of the recipient(s). As an example, in business it is the normal practice to let colleagues know about correspondence relating to matters or people that concern them. Suppose you are writing to a client on a technical matter, and you have an administrative colleague who you think needs to be informed. The technical letter, while appropriate to the client, may be virtually meaningless to the non-technical colleague. However, rather than sending a separate memo to the colleague, a few words, perhaps hand-written, on a copy of the letter, may be sufficient to convey the level of information needed by the colleague. The MD of the client company, who might also need to be informed, could be sent a copy of the technical letter, attached to another letter explaining why you think he needs to be aware of the contents and drawing his attention to particular aspects.

To INFLUENCE

* provide needed information
* buy a product or service
* pay for something already
     bought
* refund/replace defective
     item bought
* withdraw or modify a complaint
* vote for a particular candidate
* grant a request/permission/
                        interview

Figure   3.4

Figure   3.5

STRUCTURE

Any communication should have a beginning, a middle and an end. In the case of a letter, the beginning, in English, is always "Dear (Sir, Madam, Mr, Mrs, etc)" and the end is usually "Yours (faithfully, truly sincerely, etc)". If you address the correspondent by name, the end choice is usually "sincerely" or "truly"; if as "Sir" or "Madam", then use "faithfully".

The first paragraph should state the reason for the letter. If the letter is intended to *influence* the recipient, then the opening had better be brief, and of interest (not to you, to the recipient!). The middle should add to the information given in the opening and answer any questions raised there. The ending should state clearly what action you hope or expect the recipient to take as a result of your letter. Examine the sample layout of a business letter shown in Figure 3.6.

STYLE

Style is something best learned by reading. General rules are: prefer short, concrete, active words to long, abstract, passive ones. Prefer short sentences to long ones. Begin a new line of thought with a new paragraph. Above all, match vocabulary as closely as you can to what you know of the recipient's level of knowledge and education. Examine the sample letter shown in Figure 3.7.

LAYOUT

A business letter is normally sent on a printed letterhead. The layout of the printed headings may slightly affect the layout of the letter; most firms also have a 'house-style', with rules on indentation of paragraphs (see Figure 3.8) and position of date, address and complimentary close. Even if you are hand-writing on plain paper, however, decide at the outset what layout you are using and do not change half-way through.

DRAFTING A LETTER

To begin with, make notes of what you want to say, or prepare the letter itself in rough form. If you are writing on plain paper, then, unless you have a very good eye, use lined paper underneath as a guide. If you make a mistake, do not immediately start again, because you may make some more later. When you are sure about what you want to say and sure that you have found the right way of saying it, then make a final fair copy. Do not forget the date – people often do. If someone sends you an undated letter, however, do not reply "With reference to your undated letter"; "to your recent letter" is kinder.

As a final word on drafting a letter, remember that you may have your letters typed for you. In this case you should either dictate them (often on a dictaphone) or write them out for a typist to copy. If you dictate you must put yourself in the typist's place (ie relying mainly on spoken information), and state exactly where punctuation, paragraphs, etc, should go. If you hand-write your draft, it should be neat and easily read.

Layout of a business letter

1 COMPTEC LTD

2 20 Franklin Road
 Coventry
 CV1 2FE

4

3 Telephone: Coventry 462587

5 Your ref: MG/JR
 Our ref: PJ/RJ

6 8th July 1990

7 Ms J. Deed

8 Investment Department
 Coventry Finance Ltd
 West Court
 Coventry
 CV3 4WA

9 Dear Madam,

10 Expansion Programme

11 ....
 ....
 ....

12 Yours faithfully,

13

 P. Jones

14 P. Jones

15 Managing Director

16 enc.
17 Copy to: Mr. R. Thomas
18 Directors: P. Jones (Managing) S. Ross.
19 Registered office: 2 Southey Street, Birmingham B5 3AD
20 Registered number: 54682 Registered in England.

Key
1 Trading name
2 Postal address
3 Telephone number
4 Logo
5 References
6 Date
7 Recipient
8 Recipient's address
9 Greeting/salutation
10 Subject heading
11 Body of letter
12 Complimentary close
13 Signature of writer
14 Writer's name, printed (necessary for business use even if signature is clear)
15 Job description
16 Enclosure reference
17 Copy reference
18 List of directors
19 Address of registered office
20 Registered number of company and country of registration

Figure 3.6

HONEYCRISPS COMPANY LIMITED

Shawfield
Birmingham
B21 SKJ

Telephone: 021 473 2121

13th June 19..

Our ref: STJ/FJS

Dear Madam,

We were sorry to learn from your letter of 9th June 19.. that you had found a small piece of metal in your packet of Honeycrisps.

We must apologise for this occurrence. It seems that a piece of machinery became loose and small filings from it entered the packing machine. This was discovered almost immediately; however, it seems that some boxes of Honeycrisps were not checked for such foreign bodies. We are grateful that you took the trouble to contact us about this matter.

We enclose with this letter two boxes of Honeycrisps which we hope will compensate you for your distress and inconvenience.

Yours faithfully,

HONEYCRISPS CO LTD

S.T. JONES
Consumer Relations Officer

Mrs. S. Fletcher
5 Hillmeadows
Tenderham
Shrewsbury
SR3 6JT

Figure   3.7

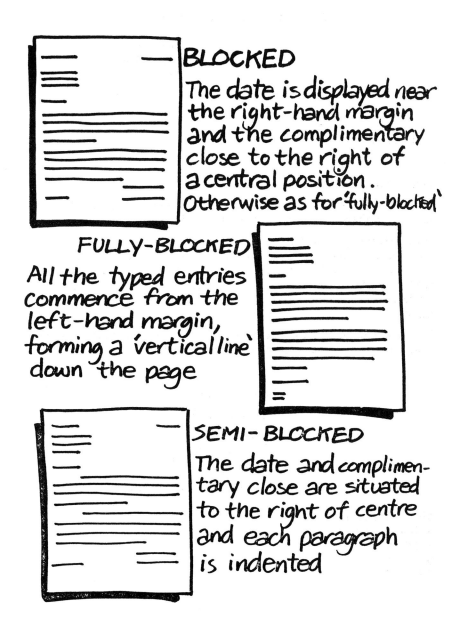

BLOCKED
The date is displayed near the right-hand margin and the complimentary close to the right of a central position. Otherwise as for 'fully-blocked'

FULLY-BLOCKED
All the typed entries commence from the left-hand margin, forming a 'vertical line' down the page

SEMI-BLOCKED
The date and complimentary close are situated to the right of centre and each paragraph is indented

Figure 3.8

REPORTS

You may from time to time be required to write a report. There are a variety of types of reports, often dependent upon the situation they are required for:

— *Routine reports* may be asked for on a regular basis, eg your progress report in school or college;
— *Occasional reports* are often written when something unusual happens, eg an accident;
— *Commissioned reports* are prepared with a specific purpose in mind. They may be required to investigate a problem that has arisen. They are commonly found in market research projects, eg on types of products or political parties.

Format

There are various possible formats, chosen according to the type of report which may run from a single sheet of paper to 100s of pages.

— *Extended formal reports* are used for important issues, often government sponsored;
— *Short formal reports* are often used as a way to communicate information between middle and senior management;
— *Short informal reports* are a useful way of conveying more minor information at lower levels within organisations. They do not require the same rigorous attention to style of layout as the more formal report.

How to Write a Short Formal Report

Probably the most useful layout to adopt is the short formal report. If the need arises for a more informal style, the formal layout can easily be modified to accommodate this.

First collect the necessary facts and take time to consider their implications, then draw your conclusions.

Sample Layout

1 Subject heading ....

2 Report's recipient .... Date ....

3 Report's author ....

4 Objectives: — what the report is about;
                — who commissioned it;
                — brief outline.

5 Research methods: how, where and when you gathered your information, eg interviews, surveys. References to any publications cited.

6 Findings: state the facts in logical order. Divide the material into numbered sections and sub-sections if necessary.

7 Conclusions: state the conclusions that you have come to having looked at all the facts. You may also state your own opinion and preferences in this section.

8 Recommendations: if you feel specific action needs to be taken, you should suggest it at this point.

Style

The style of a report should be factual and objective. As it is never possible to be wholly objective, you should always be aware that some words are more emotive than others and these should be avoided. It is only in the conclusion that you should allow any personal preference to become obvious. In order to promote objectivity in your report you should use the third person throughout, ie "It becomes evident that . . .".

Assignment

In groups choose a topic to investigate and write a report on it.

FORMS AND THEIR FUNCTION

An important aspect of written communication which needs to be considered is the use of forms. Forms are used extensively in the business world and are also encountered by individuals at nearly every juncture. They are used to record important events such as births, deaths and marriages, they must be completed in order to enrol for a course of study, apply for membership of a club, apply for a job, a driving licence, insurance, to open a bank account or to join a library – the list is endless. The use of forms seems to become more widespread every year. Many people spend much of their working lives completing (or helping others to complete) various types of forms.

Forms can be as simple or as complicated as those shown in Figures 3.9 and 3.10. These are examples of standardised documents which pose questions to elicit specific information. They are efficient in use provided their purpose has been clearly defined and provided they have been well-designed. Clear and precise instructions on its mode of completion should be an integral part of the design of every form. The primary function of a form is to efficiently gather information which, if desired, can be easily collated and analysed. A great deal of thought should go into the design and layout of a form as its effective use within

MESSAGE FORM

Time of Call _____ Date_____

Name of Caller _____

Name and Address of Firm

_____

_____

_____

Tel. No._____ Ext. No._____

Receiver of Call_____

MESSAGE ⊢————

Taken By._____

Figure   3.9

Free prescriptions

Form B – P11/April 1987

Claim on this form if you have a low income

About yourself

Surname (Mr/Mrs/Miss/Ms) ____ Date of birth ____ 19

First name(s) ____

Address ____ Postcode ____

Are you in full-time education? YES ☐ NO ☐

If you are expecting a baby, give the date it's due to be born ____ Date due ☐

Who else lives with you?

Give the names of the people in your household, their dates of birth, and say what relationship they are to you, for example, partner, parent, son, etc. Include commercial boarders.

Name	Date of birth	Relationship (state if boarder)

- If you or anybody in the list above is registered blind write their names here
- Does anybody in the list above pay you any rent? Write their names here
- Write the names of any children who are still at school full-time
- Does anybody in the list above get Supplementary Benefit? Write their names here

Your housing costs   Put a ✓ in the box that applies.

If you are a householder
- Do you own your own home? YES ☐ NO ☐
- If you have a mortgage, how much do you pay each month? £ ____
  (Take off any rebate/housing benefit)
- If you pay rent, how much do you pay each week? £ ____
  (Take off any rebate/allowance/housing benefit)
- Does the rent include heating? YES ☐ NO ☐
- How much of the rent is for heating? £ ____
- Does the rent include lighting? YES ☐ NO ☐
- How much of the rent is for lighting? £ ____

- How much do you pay each year for rates? £ ____
  (Take off any rebate/housing benefit)
- How much do you pay each year for water rates including environment and sewerage charges (if paid separately)? £ ____
- How much do you pay each year for ground rent/feu duty? £ ____

If you live in someone else's home
- What is your relationship to the householder? (If none, write NONE)
- If you live there as boarder, how much rent do you pay each week? £ ____
- Which meals are provided for you?
  Breakfast ☐   Midday ☐   Evening ☐

5

Free prescriptions

Form B – P11/April 1987

Please answer each question and write NONE where the amount is none

Money coming in

Write down the amount of take-home pay coming in each week for (if already deducted from your pay)
- yourself £
- your partner £

If you get Statutory Sick Pay or Statutory Maternity Pay, write down the amounts here for
- yourself £
- your partner £

Write down the total value of any property (don't include the home you live in or personal possessions), savings, and surrender values of life insurance policies owned by
- yourself £
- your partner £
- any dependants £

Do you or your partner get any money from benefits, pensions, or allowances? NO ☐ YES ☐
Write down which they are and say how much you get for each.
- £
- £
- £

Write down how much comes in each week from sub tenants £

Write down any other income £

Money going out

Write down how much goes out each week (not if already deducted from your pay)
- fares to work and back £
- child care costs while you are at work £
- superannuation £
- trade union subscriptions £

Write down what items you have on HP and how much your HP payments cost each week (only include essential household items)
- £
- £
- £

Write down the cost each week of any life insurance premiums
- self £
- partner/other £

Write down the name of anyone in your family who needs a special diet for health reasons and the nature of the illness
- name
- illness

If your heating bills are high because you or anyone in your family are ill and need extra heating or because your house is difficult to heat, write the reasons below.

Students. If you are in full-time further education, please attach details of your grant and of your term and vacation dates. Also show whether you are making your claim from your term-time or your vacation address.

Declaration

I declare that to the best of my knowledge and belief the information given on this form is true and complete.

Signed ____   Date ____ 19

Warning: to give false information may result in prosecution.

Cut this form from the leaflet and post it to your Social Security office. You can get a pre-paid envelope from the post office.

Figure 3.10

a company can save time and money. The overuse of forms, however, can generate a great deal of unnecessary paperwork which can lead to duplication of effort and consequently to inefficiency. Before considering the introduction of a new form the question should be asked – is it really necessary?

Designing the Form

Having taken the decision to produce a form there are several aspects which must be considered. Because of the great number and variety of forms in use, it is important that they are easily distinguishable from one another and this aspect should be taken into account when deciding on the layout. The following features might be considered:

— colour of paper;
— distinctive border;
— use of logo;
— different typefaces and type styles (eg italic, bold, etc);
— use of space (ie to produce an uncluttered layout and a variety of
  section sizes to take into account variation in answers).

Instructions on Completing the Form

Concise, clear instructions should indicate how the form is to be completed and what is to be done with it on completion, eg who should receive it; by what date, etc. It is usually helpful to state whether all sections should be completed, indicating the use of the words 'not applicable' where necessary.

The Framing of Questions

Once again clarity is all-important. Questions should be phrased in language that will be easily understood by the target group. The form will not fulfil its function if the respondent has to strive to understand the meaning of a question. All 'specialist' language should be accompanied by an explanatory note. Use can be made of direct or indirect questions, eg "How many children do you have?", "What are your domestic responsibilities?" Questions should be presented in a logical sequence. A college enrolment form, for example, might present the prospective student with a request to supply the following information: surname; forenames; address; date of birth; previous school; examination results; course required.

ASSIGNMENT 1

For this assignment you should obtain driving licence application forms from a post office.

Divide into groups. Before looking at the form, draw up a checklist of what you consider to be the most important questions the Driver and Vehicle Licensing Centre (DVLC) needs to ask a prospective driver. Put these questions in order of priority. Now look at an actual application form. Do the questions and their order conform to your checklist? If not, make a list of those questions you did not include. Do any of these surprise you? Is the form easy to understand? If not, why not?

ASSIGNMENT 2

Now that you have accustomed yourself to forms, you can practise designing your own.

Divide into groups again. Each group should represent the nucleus of a small club. This may be a leisure/sports club, eg badminton, or a hobby club, eg fantasy games. The club wishes to publicise itself in order to attract new members so it decides to distribute information leaflets about its activities with an application form for membership on the back. It is each group's task to design this form.

ASSIGNMENT 3

Examine the letter shown in Figure 3.11.

1 On the surface, this letter appears polite. Which words and phrases give this impression?

2 In fact, it is a rude letter which aims at putting Susan in the wrong. Find examples of this.

3 List all the examples of old-fashioned business jargon you can find. Do they always mean what they say?

4 Re-write the letter in such a way that the firm will not risk losing Susan's custom.

ASSIGNMENT 4

Write a letter to the Personnel Manager of 'Associated Cybernetic Systems Limited' applying for the post of trainee programmer. It is an

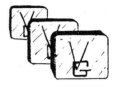

2 Low Street
Hoxley HL19 4QZ
Tel. No. Hoxley 5632

Your ref:
Our ref: JPL/MG   6th March, 1987.

Miss Susan Grant,
3 Mary Hill Road,
Toxley,
Somerset.
BAS 6LH

Dear Madam,

We are in receipt of your letter of the 28th ult. and the parcel containing the film which you returned.

We deeply regret that you failed to achieve the desired results, but would draw your attention to what we feel sure are instrumental factors in the results you describe.

1. Specific instructions are given which must be followed exactly.
2. Cameras which have not been serviced regularly will not give satisfactory results.
3. Inexperience in video filming techniques may give rise to a poor quality film, in which case, satisfactory results can hardly be expected from our film.

We must emphasise that our products are all thoroughly tested and recommended. Furthermore, we receive thousands of letters from delighted customers in praise of our goods. It is our sincere hope, therefore, that this letter has renewed your confidence in us and that you will continue to use our products in the future.

Assuring you of our best service at all times,

We remain,

Your obedient servant,

VISION GRAPHICS

J. P. Little

JOANNE P. LITTLE

Figure   3.11

IBM installation and the required programming languages are PL1 and RPG2.

The applications are a mix of scientific, for client companies, and administrative, particularly accounting, for ACSL itself. The job advertisement states that a graduate is preferred. There is a possibility of transfer into systems analysis after 2–3 years satisfactory programming, or, for an exceptional candidate, attachment to the consultancy, which operates for clients mainly in the Middle and Far East.

WORD PROCESSING

The introduction of the word processor to the office environment has not only eased the burden of the hard-pressed secretary, it has changed the environment itself. The necessity to store large quantities of paper documents in cumbersome and space-consuming filing cabinets has been very much reduced. It is now possible to retain vast quantities of information on a hard disk (incorporated into the computer), or on a number of floppy disks.

The process of information exchange via a word processor is relatively simple. Each new floppy disk needs to be formatted (a simple procedure), and then data such as letters, reports, circulars, memoranda, etc, can be inserted onto the disk and as many hard copies (printouts) as required obtained. Text can be altered with ease – the order of paragraphs, for instance, can be changed if necessary – and different print emphasis, such as the use of bold print, is readily available. It is possible, by using a process called 'mail-merge' to produce a personalised letter for circulation to the desired number of clients, however large. Filing is simplified as all information is stored on disk and, provided a security copy of each disk in use is kept, few problems should arise. The word processor facilitates both the distribution and exchange of information and has had a dramatic impact on the business world. Its full potential has yet to be realised.

4   Oral Communication

INTRODUCTION

Oral communication simply means the use of speech, but in this chapter we are concerned with one-way communication rather than the normal use of speech which is in conversation. The use of oral communication applies to many areas: you may, for instance, be asked to address a meeting, you may wish to speak from the floor of a meeting or, slightly less formally, you may have an idea or a point of view which you wish to put over to colleagues at work or fellow-members of a social group.

THE IMPORTANCE OF PREPARATION

However little time you may have for preparation, it is still important to have a plan, otherwise there is a danger that when you stop speaking your listeners will look at each other and say "What was all that about?" and you will be kicking yourself for having missed out the vital point; having failed to give it proper emphasis; repeating yourself or coming to a stop on a weak point.

You may be able to speak simply using headings that you have first noted down – but check whether these are adequate by first reading your headings into a tape recorder then playing them back. Alternatively, you may feel more comfortable if you first write out in full what you want to say. There is an obvious danger in doing this however: that you will be tempted to keep your eyes directed to your notes rather than to your audience (the easiest way to lose your audience's attention). Even if what you have to say is well-argued and interesting, it may still come across as boring if you do not appear to be interested in your audience. Also, by keeping your eyes on your audience, you are able to sense their mood and so change your style of delivery to match it. To enable you to do this, make sure that key words stand out, by using different lettering, a different colour or underlining. Keep your headings clear of the main text but see that you have enough key words so that even if you lose the thread of what you wanted to say, you can take it up again and still give an effective presentation.

THE PLAN

Introduction

Before giving a talk you will usually have been introduced by the chairman of the meeting, and you can start immediately by saying what you are going to talk about and why (see Figure 4.1). If you have not been introduced, then say who you are and what organisation you represent before moving on to your subject matter. If you are speaking from the floor in a meeting, and if a motion has been proposed, then say whether you are supporting or opposing it. If you yourself are proposing or seconding a motion, then say so.

Main Body

Your advance preparation should ensure that you have your points arranged in a logical order, with relevant arguments to support each one.

Conclusion

Summarise the important points you have been aiming to make. If the purpose of speaking is to persuade your audience of something that should be done, then end on a call for action – ask your audience to support or oppose the motion or amendment, contribute to a fund, take part in a campaign and so on. Don't just stop, and don't say something like "well, my time's up so I shall have to finish". If time was so restricted then you've wasted what you had by the time you spent on those words. (Similarly, never start by spending time saying you have not been allowed much time and so you will be very brief – it sounds like a way of passing time away and an excuse for not having anything interesting or convincing to say.)

TIMING

The most important aspect of timing is to make sure you allow yourself enough time for an effective conclusion. You should expect this to take up to a fifth of the total time. Keep a clock in view or put your watch in a place where you can see it (but do not pointedly look at the clock, or at your wrist), and note the time when you will need to begin your summing up.

REVISING

If you have prepared your notes some time before the time at which you are due to speak, it is worth checking them through again after you have

Figure 4.1

been doing something else, to be sure that you have not missed any important points and that the arrangement will allow you to make the presentation interesting. Then, as near as possible to the time at which you will be speaking, read them through again so that the contents will be fresh in your mind.

DELIVERY

If there is a chairman, then face towards him or her as you start. If you are speaking in front of an audience, turn to face them. They should feel that you are looking at each one of them and this will tend to make them feel an interest in you. Stand upright but in a relaxed way, with your weight leaning slightly forward towards the audience; do not lean away from them (Figure 4.2).

Speak up and don't mumble. It is worth pre-recording yourself and listening for any habitual speech slurring. Don't speak at one pace and on one note, otherwise you will soon have your audience snoring. Try to avoid distracting mannerisms like rattling keys or money or fiddling with spectacles. Keep your hands out of your pockets – concentrate on your subject and your hands will look after themselves. Glance at your notes when you need to: key words and phrases should be sufficiently prominent that you don't have to search for them.

Always look for audience reaction to what you are saying – the occasional *ad lib* to take advantage of these reactions can add greatly to the interest. If a member of the audience wants to ask a question, respond positively. Provided you have properly prepared your material, you should be able to capitalise on questions by giving effective answers – but be careful not to be thrown too far off your timing.

SUBJECT MATTER

If you have a choice of subject matter, then select a topic which interests you and for which you can display enthusiasm (Figure 4.3). If you don't already have the necessary knowledge, then research your subject beforehand. If you are planning to make any assertions, then make sure you have the appropriate evidence to hand, possibly with quotations.

Remember that more information tends to be taken in through the eyes than through the ears, so if there is something relevant that you can give the audience to look at – so long as it supports what you are saying and is not distracting – then any time spent in the preparation of visuals will not be wasted. Even something that the audience can't see can arouse interest, as for instance if you hold up a document which illustrates or emphasises your point and say: "I have in my hand the following . . .".

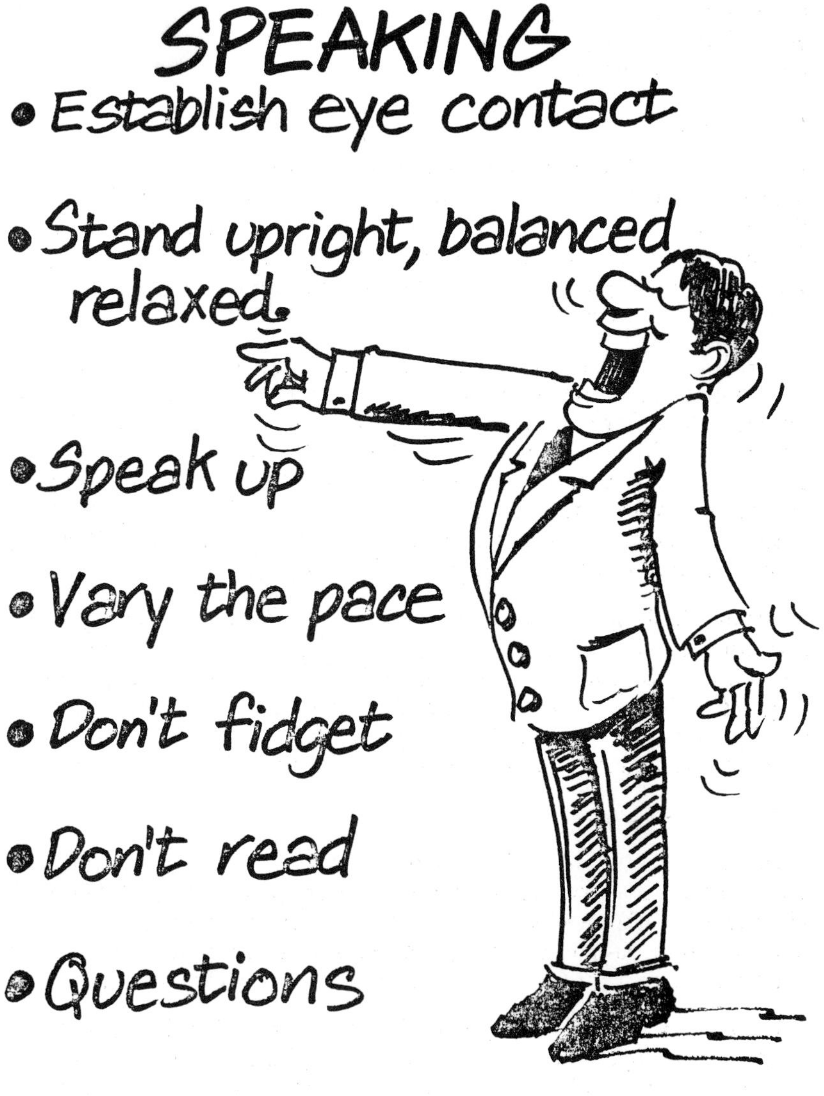
SPEAKING
• Establish eye contact
• Stand upright, balanced relaxed.
• Speak up
• Vary the pace
• Don't fidget
• Don't read
• Questions

Figure 4.2

Figure   4.3

ASSIGNMENT

Materials needed: cards with names of characters and roles.

Student activity: — drawing up an agenda;
— taking minutes;
— presenting speech to meeting.

You are presented with a hypothetical situation, eg a proposal to build a motorway in your area. You are each provided with a card and expected to take on the role it describes. You must prepare a 3-minute speech from the information given on the card. However, you may bring in any extra points which seem to be relevant. You must then present this speech at a simulated formal meeting. Other students will act as an audience and they must be prepared to ask questions (which you must then answer), and to take part in a discussion. Students should also draw up an agenda and take minutes of this meeting.

If possible, these speeches should be filmed and played back so that students can assess their own performance.

Assessment Criteria

Speech and discussion – possible score 85%.

Mark for: the ability to present a clear and well structured speech; clarity of voice; organisation of content and an understanding of the conventions of a formal meeting.

A credit grade should be given to students who show insight into the situation – who attempt to use the vocabulary and attitudes of the role given to them and who bring in sensible background detail. They should also show diplomacy in handling opposition to their viewpoint both in their speech and in the subsequent discussion.

A fail should be given to students whose speech in incoherent, who have made no effort to enter realistically into the role and who make no attempt to enter into the discussion.

Agenda and minutes – possible score 15%.

Students should show a knowledge of the formal rules and terminology of drawing up agenda and minutes. They should show ability to select main points from the meeting for inclusion in their minutes.

THE ASSESSMENT PROCESS

Introduction

— Did the talk have a title and was it made clear at the outset how much of the subject would be covered?
— Was the introduction sufficient to enable the listener to follow the theme of the talk?
— Did the speaker try to create interest in his subject?
— Was enthusiasm for the subject displayed?

Presentation

— Was material presented well or badly?
— Was material arranged in logical sequence or was it disjointed?
— Did the speaker show a knowledge of the subject?
— Did the talk show evidence of research?
— Did the talk have a *beginning*, a *middle* and an *end*?
— Did the speaker show any defects in presentation?
— Was the speaker fluent? (ie were such expressions as '-er', 'you know', etc, avoided?)
— Was the overall pace too fast or too slow?
— Were there variations of speed?
— Was there a variety of intonation and style?
— Were there any distracting mannerisms?
— Did the speaker try to display confidence?
— Did the speaker try to establish eye contact with audience?
— Did the speaker try to use any visual aids to assist in his or her presentation?
— Was the speaker capable of competently handling questions from members of the audience?
— What was your overall impression?

Evaluation Table

	Un-acceptable	Weak	Acceptable	Good	Very good
Preparation: **Knowledge of/analysis of problem** Knowledge of background Knowledge of audience Arrangement of facilities (ie suitable room, visual aids)					
Comments:					
Presentation: Personal — appearance — manner — vocal clarity — vocal modulation					
Comments: Material — introduction — findings — conclusions — summary of recommendations — detailed recommendations — final conclusion, if any					
Comments: *Overall reaction:* Awareness of audience Reaction to feedback Opportunity for questions					
Comments:					
Final grading on overall impressions:					

TELEPHONE TECHNIQUE

Answering the telephone is an important duty because when you are working in an office you are representing your firm and the tone of your greeting and the manner in which you handle the calls create a favourable or unfavourable first impression.

Telephone Systems

There are three main kinds of telephone system and various inter-connecting devices which facilitate the task of oral communication by telephone.

Internal

On internal telephones you are able only to talk to people inside the firm by means of another telephone extension. You cannot make outside (external) telephone calls.

External

On external telephones, you can dial external telephone numbers only.

Both

On some telephone systems you can dial internal extensions as above, but if you have to make an external call you are able to get an outside line. Often this is done by first dialling 9 to connect you to the dialling tone for the outside line.

Switchboards

In a firm which has several extensions a switchboard is necessary to receive and route the incoming calls to the required person or department. There are two main types:

PMBX – an abbreviation for private manual branch exchange – is a system in which the telephonist makes all the connections between the extension users and the incoming and outgoing calls.

PABX – an abbreviation for private automatic branch exchange – is a system whereby the extension users may dial their own calls; the switchboard operator, however, must receive and route incoming calls.

Answering Machines

If you wish to provide a 24-hour telephone service you may connect the telephone to an answering machine. This gives a pre-recorded announcement asking the caller to record a message on tape.

Task 1

Find out what types of telephones your college uses. How do you make an external telephone call from the college? Find out what type of switchboard is used.

Task 2

You are asked to ring a local florists to order flowers for the manager's office. When you telephone, you hear a recorded message which says: "Bournville Florists. Thank you for your call. The shop is closed for lunch. If you wish to leave a message it will be dealt with this afternoon. Please give your name, address and telephone number and speak slowly and clearly. Begin your message now . . ."

Write down the message you would leave, making your answer clear and concise.

Task 3

Find out how many telephone reference books there are and what their specialities are.

Look in the front pages of your local telephone directory and find the names of the recorded services available to subscribers. Find the telephone number of each recorded service (the centre nearest to you) and work out the cost for a one minute call to each one.

Find the following telephone numbers:

— the local bus or coach station;
— the nearest main line train station;
— the local library;
— the nearest information centre;
— the local police station.

What number should one dial in an emergency? Name the emergency services.

Operating the Telephone

Before you begin to dial a number you should make a note of all the information you may need in order to make an efficient telephone call. Be prepared for various turns in the conversation and collect your thoughts and all necessary paperwork beforehand. The telephone call record shown on page 87 gives an example of a useful information planning memo that you may want to use. When you are ready, make your telephone call keeping in mind the following points:

— make sure you have the correct number and dial carefully;

— try to make long distance calls during the cheap rate periods if they are not urgent;

— do not agree to hang on if you cannot be put through straight away;

— keep the conversation brief, concise and to the point.

Speak clearly when making or receiving a call. When answering the phone always say 'Good Morning' or 'Good Afternoon' as appropriate and state the name of your company. Never be too familiar with the telephone callers or too rude. For example, if the person who your caller wants is out, neither have a long chatty discussion about it nor dismiss their enquiry with a curt 'He/She's out'. The polite response is to ask if you can take a message. For this reason it is always useful to keep a pen and a message pad by the telephone and to observe the following list of appropriate responses:

— answer promptly;

— find out who the caller wants to speak to;

— do not leave the caller waiting without informing him/her of what action you are taking to connect him/her;

— always be polite, sympathetic and remain calm, even if subject to verbal abuse;

— if you cannot connect the caller immediately, offer him/her a choice of actions, such as to be phoned back later (meanwhile take a note of the caller's telephone number); to be connected to an alternative person likely to be of assistance; to leave a message.

Task 4

Arrange with your tutor to make an internal phone call. You wish to telephone Mr Lynch, the Environmental Health Officer, to ask him to come and advise the staff about what to do about a wasps' nest that has been found just outside the main entrance. After you have made this call to your tutor record the appropriate details in the 'Telephone Call Record' given in Figure 4.4.

TELEPHONE CALL RECORD

date + time of call	
name + address of organisation	
telephone number	
extension	
name of person you want to speak to	
your name	
where you are from	
why you are phoning	
what you want to know	
information obtained	

Figure   4.4

5 Applying for a Job

LETTER OF APPLICATION

One letter, the one that lands you your first job, can totally change your life, so never let an application go until you are satisfied that you cannot improve upon it.

The Sifting Process

Put yourself in the position of the employer who has just advertised a vacancy; the letters start pouring in. There could be 20 or 200 letters of application for a single job. Out of all of these, the employer has to pick just 5 or 10 to ask to an interview. What would *you* do? How would *you* pick out the small handful which 'win' at this stage of the competition, and get invited to an interview? Let us look at ways in which you can try to get your own letter among the winners.

The First Throw-out

To begin with the employer does not think about the 'good' letters. His first interest is the *bad ones* – the ones he can throw straight into the bin. Firstly he will throw out any letters that are dirty and badly written. Remember, he *wants* to find an excuse for throwing all but a handful away, so any excuse will be pounced on and that letter will end up in the rubbish bin (see Figure 5.1).

The Second Throw-out

An employer will then go through the letters again, throwing out some more, until he has about twice the number that he wants to interview left. At this stage, he will keep only the letters which satisfy the following criteria:

— they are not too long;
— they give relevant information about the applicant;
— they avoid any attempt to show off;
— they do not waffle or give unnecessary information.

Figure 5.1

Short List

Finally, the employer will go through the pile a third time, and this time he will be looking for something positive, that certain 'something' that says "This person seems to be good. He (or she) seems to be the kind of person we ought to ask to an interview".

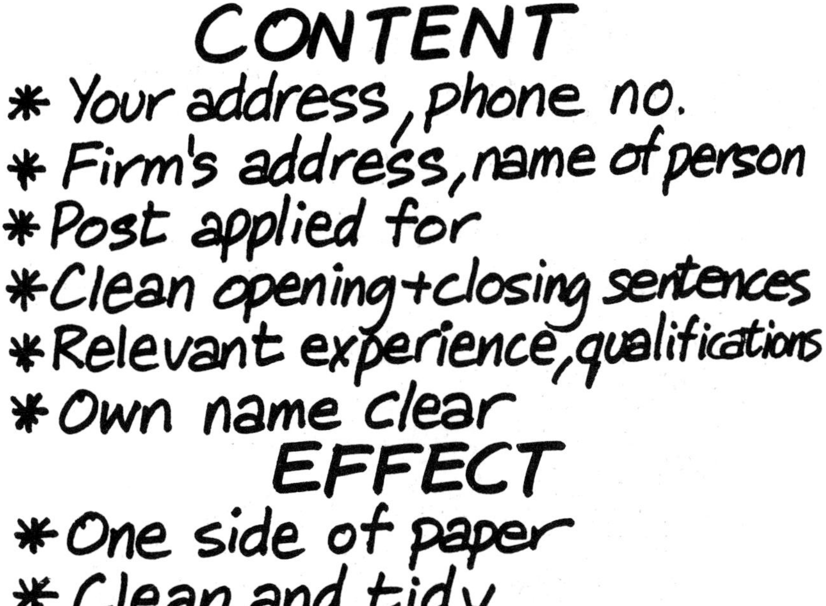

CONTENT

* Your address, phone no.
* Firm's address, name of person
* Post applied for
* Clean opening + closing sentences
* Relevant experience, qualifications
* Own name clear

EFFECT

* One side of paper
* Clean and tidy

Figure 5.2

The Essentials

So how do you avoid both the 'throw-out' stages shown above and get through to the short list (Figure 5.2)? Many letters of application miss the most obvious points – even the applicant's address. Make sure you include all the following essentials:

— the address where you can normally be contacted, at the top, with a phone number if possible;
— the date;
— the address of the firm you are writing to;
— if you know the name of the person you are writing to then either address him or her directly or put 'For the attention of Mr/Mrs/Ms . . .';
— indicate the post you are applying for;
— give clear opening and closing sentences;
— give details of previous experience and employment – perhaps in the form of a separate curriculum vitae (see below);
— show how you can meet the stated and hidden requirements of the
— job (but do not apologise for experience or qualifications you *do not* have);
— keep it short. If your application letter is too long employers might not read it at all. Avoid unnecessary details such as hobbies, religion, previous salary, reasons for leaving the last job, etc, unless they are specifically asked for. Include only the things that would interest *you* if you were the employer. Aim to fill one side of an A4 sheet of paper and no more;
— print your name underneath your signature.

Make sure the whole letter is clean, clear and tidy, without any crossings out or mistakes. When you make your first mistake do not begin the letter again; keep going because you are bound to spot other weaknesses; so let your first attempt be the rough version. Study the checklist shown in Figure 5.3 before trying to compose your letter.

APPLICATION FORMS

Some employers may require you to fill in an application form like the one shown in Figure 5.4. If an advertisement specifies this, simply write or phone for the application form and fill it in rather than wasting your efforts composing a letter of application. As an exercise, read the form carefully, then fill it in.

The Questions

Some of the questions on a printed application form may seem pointless – your hobbies, for instance, or whether you are married. You must assume that the employer has a purpose in asking them, and if you want the job, it is no use picking a quarrel about it at this stage!

Experience and Education

Application forms usually allow a certain amount of space for these

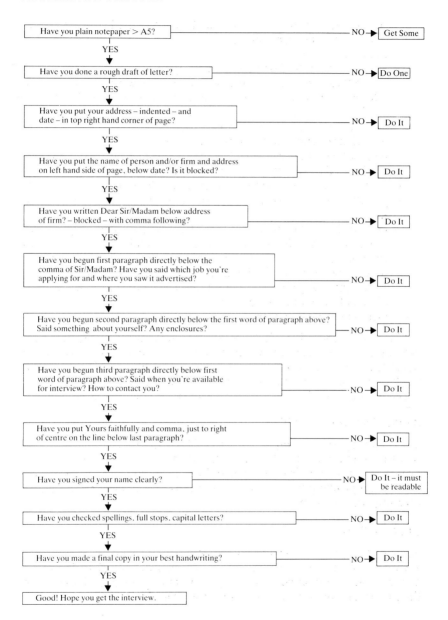

Have you plain notepaper > A5? — NO → Get Some

YES ↓

Have you done a rough draft of letter? — NO → Do One

YES ↓

Have you put your address – indented – and date – in top right hand corner of page? — NO → Do It

YES ↓

Have you put the name of person and/or firm and address on left hand side of page, below date? Is it blocked? — NO → Do It

YES ↓

Have you written Dear Sir/Madam below address of firm? – blocked – with comma following? — NO → Do It

YES ↓

Have you begun first paragraph directly below the comma of Sir/Madam? Have you said which job you're applying for and where you saw it advertised? — NO → Do It

YES ↓

Have you begun second paragraph directly below the first word of paragraph above? Said something about yourself? Any enclosures? — NO → Do It

YES ↓

Have you begun third paragraph directly below first word of paragraph above? Said when you're available for interview? How to contact you? — NO → Do It

YES ↓

Have you put Yours faithfully and comma, just to right of centre on the line below last paragraph? — NO → Do It

YES ↓

Have you signed your name clearly? — NO → Do It – it must be readable

YES ↓

Have you checked spellings, full stops, capital letters? — NO → Do It

YES ↓

Have you made a final copy in your best handwriting? — NO → Do It

YES ↓

Good! Hope you get the interview.

Figure 5.3

APPLICATION

FORM

Surname (BLOCK LETTERS)

Christian name(s) in full

Full Postal Address
(BLOCK LETTERS)

Date of birth   Note: You will be required to produce
                                                                a birth certificate.

Married or single | Nationality

Full time education

Date		Name and type of school	Standard reached, examinations passed
from	to		

Training Give details of courses taken since full time education ceased

Date		College	Subject and Qualification	Type of Course
from	to			

Figure 5.4

Full particulars of your Employment over the last 4 years

Names and addresses of Employers	Dates		Duties	Reason for leaving
	from	to		

Health   Office use only

Have you suffered from —	
fits	
rupture	
any other serious illness	
any accident	
If registered under The Disabled Persons Act 1944 give Registered No.	

Leisure interests (hobbies, sports, clubs etc.)

The information I have given above is true to the best of my knowledge
and belief.

Signed _____   Date _____

For official use

Suitability (Tick appropriate box.)	highly suitable
	probably suitable
	suitable
	unsuitable

comments covering experience, special qualities etc.

Figure   5.4a

details. First see what is required, then write it out on scrap paper to make sure you have the information in the correct order and that you will be able to fit it into the space available. Remember the importance of 'first impressions'.

Appearance

Write neatly using pen, not pencil. Print if your normal writing is uneven or untidy. If the form says 'use capitals', then make sure you do.

Completeness and Correct Spelling

Ask someone else to check your completed application form before sending it in. It is easy to miss something out without noticing. Employers also place a lot of importance on correct spelling – even judging poor spelling to be an indication of low intelligence – something which is not necessarily the case.

Completion of an Application Form at the Employers' Premises

If you know you are going to have to fill in a form when you arrive for interview, prepare a CV beforehand then have it checked as above. Carefully check your entries on the form against those of the original before handing the form in. Your CV will also serve as a source of information to ensure that you have missed out nothing important.

Why You Want the Job

Application forms may contain a section asking for further relevant information about yourself and about your reasons for wanting the job. You should think carefully about how your abilities, interests, training and experience match the needs of the job, and why you want the job. Those who make the best of this opportunity are the ones most likely to be invited to an interview.

CURRICULUM VITAE

In order to keep a letter of application short and readable, it can be a good idea to prepare a separate CV. It will also save you a lot of work if you need to apply for several jobs before you get a firm offer. Make sure the CV is clearly laid out and keep its length to two sides of a page at most – one side is preferable (see Figure 5.5).

EXERCISE 1

Prepare your own CV using the suggested layout given in Figure 5.5.

CURRICULUM VITAE

Name:

Address:

Tel No:

Date of birth:

Age: (in years)

Sex:

Status: Single/Married

Education:

_____	School	Year – Year
_____	College	Year – Year
_____	University	Year – Year

Qualifications:

CSEs   Subject   Grade   Subject   Grade
      ”   ”   ”   ”
      ”   ”   ”   ”

'O' Levels   Subject   Grade   Subject   Grade
      ”   ”   ”   ”
      ”   ”   ”   ”

'A' Levels   Subject   Grade   Subject   Grade
      ”   ”   ”   ”
      ”   ”   ”   ”

Degree(s) or other post-school qualifications:

Postgraduate qualifications:

Work Experience:

Full-time work:
1) Position   Firm   Date – Date
2)   ”
3)   ”

Part-time work:
1) Position   Firm   Date – Date

Hobbies and Interests:

Referees:

Academic: **Character:**
Name   Name
Position   Position
Address   Address

Tel No.   Tel No.

Figure 5.5

EXERCISE 2

1 If possible, work in groups of 5 or 6.

Pretend you are the bosses. You are going to choose a new employee for your firm. Decide what kind of job it is and what the new person will have to do. When you have done this, prepare an advertisement for the rest of the class to respond to.

Here are some words you might need:

applicant	permanent	confidence
qualifications	temporary	proficient
experience	competent	enthusiastic
clerical	assistant	position

When you have finished one member of your group's 'Board of Directors' should write your advertisement on the blackboard.

2 Everyone in the class should now write letters of application for the jobs advertised by the different groups. If possible write applications for two or three different jobs. *Use false names throughout* so that each application can be judged on its merits. Send your letters.

3 Each 'Board of Directors' now sorts the applications for 'your' advertisement to decide which applicant you want to interview – you should also choose one 'reserve' candidate.

4 Under the heading 'HOW WE CHOSE OUR CANDIDATE', answer the following questions:

— What made you choose your 'best' candidate – his or her age; qualifications; handwriting; address; interests; some other factor?
— What made you reject some of the candidates – their handwriting; spelling mistakes; length of letter; an obvious inaccuracy; some other factor?
— Make some suggestions for things an employer would look for when he reads a letter of application, and how he would choose his short list.

5 Now decide on a job you wish to apply for from the suggestions already given and try writing the most honest letter about yourself that you can manage. The letter should be as from a school-leaver applying for a first job.

Points to remember:

— Set the letter out carefully, with your address and the date at the top right hand corner and the address of the company on the left hand side below yours. Begin 'Dear Sir or Madam'.
— Paragraph your letter carefully.

Introduction – say what position you are applying for, and how you came to know about the vacancy.

Main part – give the most important points about yourself – age, school, examinations you have taken or are studying for, when you will be available, skills, hobbies, interests, and full- or part-time work experience. Use the 'Personal Profile' checklist given in Figure 5.6.

Conclusion – say why you are specially interested in the job you are applying for. Request an interview. End with 'Yours faithfully'.

Personal Profile Checklist

Use this checklist each time you write a letter of application. Do not post the application until you have put a tick by *every* point.

FIRST HURDLE:	Clean sheet of paper, larger than A5, unlined; straight margin, straight lines; clean and tidy appearance, no crossings out; correct spelling and grammar; clean envelope, 1st class stamp.
SECOND HURDLE:	Short and to the point; orderly presentation; relevant details about your experience and qualifications; no irrelevant personal details; no mention of previous salary; no mention why you left your last job; something to suggest you have noticed and can meet the 'hidden requirements'.
THIRD HURDLE:	An overall calm and confident impression; something to imply that you are hard-working, responsible, etc; something to make the employer think 'I must see this person to find out more'.

SPELLING HINTS:

Personnel	Advertisement	Assistant
Experience	Responsible	Opportunity
Sincerely	Appropriate	Requirements
Faithfully	Relevant	

Figure 5.6

WHICH ONE GETS THE JOB?

Writing a letter of application for a job requires a great deal of skill. You need to be as brief as possible but nevertheless make sure that you have included all the relevant details. The following is an example of a job advertisement and three letters of application for the post (Figures 5.7, a, b and c). Read all four carefully then answer the questions that follow.

Wanted – Sales representative for newly-established computer software firm. Apply, giving details of age, education and experience, with the names and addresses of two referees to: Personnel Manager, Rampart Ltd, Snowhill, Surrey S22 3EQ.

10 Beecham Croft,
Epsom,
Surrey.
S41 0HD

15th May, 19..

Personnel Manager,
Rampart Ltd.,
Snowhill,
Surrey.

S22 3EQ

Dear Sir,
    I wish to apply for the position of sales representative. I am 21 years of age and was educated at Hilltop Grammar School.
    I am employed as a sales representative with Staines Ltd. I would require a salary of at least £10,000 per year. My references are P. Richards, Esq., 40 Grove Street, Moorcroft and J. L. Pierce, Esq., Longacre Road, Littletown, Surrey.

Yours faithfully,

James Smith

JAMES SMITH

Figure 5.7a

75 Green Lane,
Sunnyside,
Surrey.
S43 9AD

15th May, 19..

Personnel Manager,
Rampart Ltd.,
Snowhill,
Surrey.
S22 3EQ

Dear Sir,

Your advertisement for a sales representative in the 'Snowhill Echo' was just what I have been looking for. I have long admired your very successful company and would welcome the chance to work for it.

I went to school at Snowhill Comprehensive School, which I left in 1983. The teachers all seemed to like me and I always had a good school report.

My first job was with Snowhill Electronics, but their sales methods were not dynamic enough for me so I left. I am working for Peter Green now where the work is far more exciting.

I consider with my valuable experience that I should expect a reasonably high salary, but we can discuss that at the interview.

Perhaps I should have mentioned that I was picked for the Surrey under 15's rugby team while at school, but I felt it would take too much of my time and so I withdrew after one season.

I have chosen two very honest and well-respected members of the Snowhill community as my referees. The first is Ms N Hill, a solicitor and a J. P. Her address is, The Grange, Littletown Road, Snowhill, Surrey. The second is my uncle, Sam Smythe, a local Tory councillor who I'm sure you've seen canvassing around Snowhill town centre at the beginning of May. His address is Stoneycroft Lodge, Smallheath, Snowhill, Surrey.

I should do my utmost to please you if I got this job and I look forward with much pleasure to meeting you at the interview.

Yours faithfully,

PAUL BACON

Figure   5.7b

43 Carlton Mews,
Castletown,
Surrey.
S32 0AD

15th May, 19..

Personnel Manager,
Rampart Ltd.,
Snowhill,
Surrey.
S22 3EQ

Dear Sir,
        I wish to apply for the post of sales representative advertised
in the current issue of the 'Snowhill Echo'. I am twenty-two years of age
and was educated at Littletown Comprehensive School, where I took
three A levels and seven O levels, including A levels in both
Mathematics and Computer Studies.

        Since leaving school in 1983 I have been employed by
Roberts & Co. Ltd., first as a trainee salesman, then later as a computer
salesman for the south-west area. Unfortunately I feel I must leave now
as there are few opportunities for promotion.

        The referees I should like to offer are my sales manager and
my former headmaster. Their addresses are, J. Holt, Esq., Sales
Manager, Roberts & Company Ltd., Snowhill, Surrey and S. Ryman,
Esq., Littletown Comprehensive School, Littletown, Surrey.

        I currently earn £8,000 per annum and I should expect a
similar starting salary. However, I am aware that many companies now
prefer to pay on a salary plus commission basis and I would be prepared
to consider this arrangement at any interview which you care to arrange.

                        Yours faithfully

                        PHILIP TIMMS

Figure   5.7c

EXERCISE 3

Questions

1 The advertisement asks specifically for four items of information. Which of the writers has completely ignored the first of these?

2 What criticism could be made of the referees offered by James Smith?

3 Which writer has given the most useful account of his education?

4 Who has given no real estimate of the salary he expects?

5 Who is guilty of the fault of irrelevancy? Quote one example from his letter.

6 Do you consider the details given by James Smith about his experience sufficient for the purpose? If not, what other information would you have liked to see?

7 Who has marshalled his facts so badly that one piece of important information is put in as an afterthought?

8 If you had to judge on the letters alone, to which one would you give the job?

9 Write a short criticism of the other two letters.

EXERCISE 4

Carefully avoiding all the faults you have just been criticising, write a letter applying for the following post:

Wanted, clerk (male or female) for postal sales firm. Typing essential. Write in first instance, giving details of age, education, experience and proof of further education since leaving school, together with the names and addresses of two referees to Personnel Officer, Branda Ltd, Dunmouth, Cumberland.

6 Interviewing and Being Interviewed

PREPARATION

The Job

What type of skill is required?
What are the normal working hours?
Where will you normally be working?
Will you need training?
Will your workmates be your own age or much older?

Questions to Ask

Decide what is most important to you in a job:

Is length of holiday important?
Is freedom of choice important?
Do you need quiet surroundings?
Do you want the chance to earn overtime or extra pay – for instance shift allowance?
Is a canteen, or sporting or other facilities important?

Know Yourself

Think about what you are really like:

What are you good at?
What *don't* you like doing?
What are your hobbies and interests?
How do you compare with the person the employer is asking for?

THE INTERVIEW

An interview is a two-way exchange. You are looking for a job, and the employer is looking for someone to fill a vacancy. Neither of you is doing the other a favour. Some interviewers have training and experience in interviewing but you may well find yourself being interviewed by someone who is as inexperienced at interviewing as you are at being interviewed. You will then have to help each other.

An interview is a highly unnatural kind of meeting. You might as well recognise this, and present yourself for it in an unnaturally clean and conventionally dressed state. You may well see computer operators dressed in jeans and casual shirts, but, if you arrive dressed like that, you will immediately lose points with the interviewer. You may normally sit down in any company, or light up a cigarette, without being asked, but not in an interview. Do not arrive chewing gum, and try to avoid off-putting habits such as picking your nose.

If your letter of application or application form has done its job properly, the interviewer already has a lot of factual information about you, about what you have done and about what you enjoy doing; what he needs to discover at the interview is what sort of person you are. He can only do this if you are prepared to talk about yourself. If you have taken advantage of the opportunity presented by the letter of application or application form, the direction of the questions put by the interviewer will be those aspects of yourself, and of your activities, that you will enjoy talking about, and about which you can talk knowledgeably and intelligently. So many people fail at an interview because the two parties fail to discover any common ground, and so the interview becomes a series of mutually boring interchanges. Make sure, then, that whatever you have entered earlier about your achievements and interests, you can proceed to give a good account of at the actual interview. If you can start talking about something that really interests you, the real you can then become apparent, in spite of the artificial situation you find yourself in.

Interviewers are trained to ask questions which cannot be answered by a simple yes or no. This form of questioning is a deliberate effort to get the interviewee talking. However, if your interviewer betrays a lack of training by asking questions which could be answered by a simple yes or no, you can take the initiative by saying something like 'usually, but . . .' or 'yes, unless . . .', or even 'it depends what you mean by . . .'.

An interviewer will usually ask you, probably towards the end of the interview, whether there are any questions *you* want to ask. This is your opportunity to show what a keen, critical mind you have, but you would have to be very bright to produce intelligent questions at that moment. Do ask about the firm, its products, customers and systems, and about the prospects for promotion, travel, etc. Do not ask about holidays, discount purchases, length of lunch breaks, etc.

In the end, however capable, experienced and qualified you may be, the interviewer, if he is your prospective manager, wants to know how well you and he will get along (and, of course, you need to form an opinion of that as well). The only evidence for this is how you look and what you say; even though you may find a particular subject intensely interesting, look for a response in the face of the interviewer, and, if you see any sign of boredom there, bring what you are saying to a quick conclusion and give him a chance to change the subject to one that interests him. If you should get a really bad interviewer, who does most of the talking and bores you, if you want that job try not to *show* how bored you are. You will probably spend relatively little time in the company of your manager once you have the job, and to be bored for half an hour in order to get the job you want is a small price to pay.

Summing Up Interview Technique

— Think forward to the interview at the time you make the written application;
— arrive on time, clean and conventionally dressed;
— wait to be asked before you sit down, or light up a cigarette. Sit upright, but not stiffly with your arms folded over-defensively;
— take any opportunity given by the questions to talk on a subject which interests you, so long as you are sure it is not boring the interviewer;
— prepare yourself with one or two sensible questions for use if the opportunity presents itself;
— when leaving, thank the interviewer for seeing you;
— there is no perfect recipe for getting a job, but, if you can express yourself well, both in writing and in speech, and can look and sound pleasant, your chances will be greatly increased. As a preparation, study the questions listed in Figure 6.1.

THE APPOINTMENT BOARD

You may well find yourself in front of not one interviewer, but a board of anything from six to twenty people. This can be an unnerving experience if you have not prepared for it.

In order to do this you should take turns with a partner at being the interviewee and a member of the board. If you are the candidate you should have a sheaf of information about the job to help you prepare. If you are a member of the board you should receive information about the job and the role you are to play during the interview (see Figures 6.2 and 6.3). Subsequently, you should be able to view and criticise your own performance, and then if time permits, try again, with different people in the different roles.

ASSIGNMENT 1
Questions for Candidates

Imagine that you have just applied for a job which you are interested in. Take a look at the questions listed below, some of which you may be asked when you go for an interview. Prepare yourself for the interview by writing some answers to these questions.

Which subjects did you like best at school?_____

Why?_____

Which subject are you best at?_____

Why?_____

Do you have any special hobbies or interests?_____

Have you taken any exam(s)? How well do you think you did in it (them)?

_____

How did you hear about this job?_____

Why do you want to do this particular sort of work?_____

What do you know about this firm?_____

_____

There follows a short list of questions which you may find useful to ask at the interview. Tick the three you consider to be the most important and add any others you feel are also important.

What sort of things will I be doing in this job?

What sort of training will I receive?

What sort of hours will I have to work?

What is the rate of pay and what kinds of 'stoppages' are there?

Will I have to work during evenings or weekends?

Will I need any special clothing or tools?

If I'm offered the job, can I see where I would be working?

If I do well in the job, where can it lead in terms of career development?

What sort of people will I be working with?

Figure   6.1

Points for Interviewers

1 Consider the job.

2 Consider the experience and formal qualifications required.

3 Consider the personal qualities required to carry out the job.

4 Reduce the basic qualifications to no more than 4 or 5.

5 Discuss with other selectors.

6 Consider the application in the light of the formal qualifications, experience and age of applicant.

7 Consider the application in the light of the qualities required.

8 Consider the application in order to find the 'common link' with the candidate in front of you.

9 Verify any unexplained gaps in dates.

10 Arrange to eliminate or reduce interruptions during the interview.

11 Arrange the seating so that neither interviewer nor candidate is at a disadvantage.

12 Examine your own prejudices.

13 Make it immediately clear to the candidate where he/she is to sit, deposit coat, etc.

14 Adopt a 'common link' approach or an 'off balance' approach or a mixture of the two.

15 Try to keep silent so that the candidate gets a fair hearing.

16 Head straight into the groups of subjects you want to discuss.

17 Avoid asking any 'yes/no' questions.

18 Question the candidate with the purpose of eliciting information.

19 Try to get at the truth by indirect questioning if necessary.

20 Follow up the candidate's opinions thoroughly.

21 Avoid any tendency to 'trick' the candidate.

22 Explain the job and its terms and conditions.

23 Tell the candidate when interview results will be made known.

24 Consider evidence from the candidate's past only as pointers.

25 Add your own impressions to what you have heard.

26 Make up your mind.

Figure   6.2

Interview Sheet (for use by interviewers)

Name of Candidate _____   Date of Interview _____

	Excellent	Above average	Average	Below average	Poor
Physical make-up					
Attainment					
Education					
Training					
Experience					
General Intelligence					
Special Aptitudes					
Words					
Figures					
Manual dexterity					
Mechanical aptitude					
Interests					
Social					
Practical					
Active (physically)					
Artistic					
Disposition					
How well does he/she get on with other people?					
Does he/she influence them?					
Is he/she self-reliant?					
Is he/she dependable?					
Circumstances					
Early background					
Present background					
Wife/Husband					
Family					

Figure   6.3

ASSIGNMENT 2

Notes for Participants

This assignment aims to explore the roles of interviewer and inter-viewee.

The assignment scenario involves a vacancy for a principal at Welling College of Further Education. The college is situated in a quiet, old-fashioned, medium-sized town and occupies an area surrounded by rundown buildings. Three miles to the south is a secondary school with a small sixth form. The parents of students at the school are mostly professional people and there is strong support for the parents' association which has successfully raised money to finance facilities such as a new computer laboratory.

The vacancy has arisen because the outgoing principal has reached retirement age. She has held her position for the last twenty years and has recently expressed concern about the role of the college in the town. Until recently the local school has shared the post-16 education, but because of falling birthrate there are fewer students now and more and more of them are choosing to stay on at the school rather than come to the college.

The outgoing principal gave an address to staff during her final year. A copy of this document is available to applicants for the post (see below).

In order to complete this assignment you should choose to be either a candidate or a member of the appointments board. Choose a false name in both instances in order to ensure an unprejudiced assessment. You will be given details of your 'character' (see page 112 for board members; page 113 for candidates), which you may expand upon but may not change. You may make notes from the details and then hand them back to your lecturer.

Copy of Principal's Address

Welcome to the College. I know that there has been a great deal of pressure on staff this year because of staff cuts, and an increased burden of work especially on courses designed for the lower ability groups. May I say that I hope to be able to announce the provision of five new appointments for the coming year which should ease some of the pressure. However, it is up to us to pull together and work as a team, not to dwell on problems and blow them up out of all proportion. Perhaps we can then steer our college through these difficult times to a better future.

Our greatest problem is in attracting the right calibre of student. As you know, Welling Comprehensive School has been steadily developing its A level work. It has had tremendous support from its parents who have, amongst other facilities, just set up a computer workroom. We do not have a strong parents' association to raise money for such facilities and this obviously puts us at a disadvantage. However, I feel that we can still attract students with our well-recognised expertise in the more traditional courses in the Humanities. It is on developing these subjects that I propose we should concentrate our energies in the coming year. Thank you.

Chairperson of the Appointments Board

I represent the County Education Authority. It is my responsibility to introduce the members of the board to the candidate, to ask him or her the opening question and at the end of the interview to ask whether he/she wishes to ask any questions of the board.

The County Education Authority would be pleased to see a younger, more dynamic person take over as principal of the college. The outgoing principal was very keen to compete with the local school but was not prepared to consider changing her very traditional concept of education. We should, however, expect any prospective candidate to have thoroughly worked out any new initiative he or she might want to introduce.

As Chairperson of this board it is important that I make sure that every member of the board gets a chance to ask a question and that no one member gets to ask too many questions. I aim not to offer my own opinion unless the other members of the board cannot agree.

Board Member I

I am a staff member and a member of the Board of Governors of Welling College. I am looking for a candidate who will 'sweep away the cobwebs' left by our departing principal. In my view a new principal should be able to start afresh and give staff the opportunity to change some of the more old-fashioned courses. This college has gradually grown less attractive to prospective students because it has not kept up with new initiatives in education. Students nowadays want 'high-tech' courses, not traditional subjects such as English and History. I certainly will not stay at this college for much longer if the new principal does not move with the times, and I know that many of my colleagues agree with me.

Board Member II

I am a local councillor and I run my own small printing business. I really have no definite preference about the educational views of any new principal. As a business man myself I consider the job of a principal to be primarily one of management. A college such as this one has a large teaching and administrative staff. It is important that everyone feels that their roles in the college are being considered and that they feel they are not merely 'cogs in a wheel'.

I also think that a principal should be able to market his or her product – the college – and should encourage private enterprise to take advantage of courses whose content could increase their communication skills.

I will be looking for a candidate who has had some experience in the commercial world. However, in terms of candidates' educational views, I shall defer to members of the board who have some educational expertise.

Board Member III

I am a local magistrate, headteacher of Welling Primary School and a member of the Board of Governors of Welling College. As someone in the teaching profession myself I am keen to see educational standards upheld. These days there are far too many 'trendy' ideas infiltrating our educational establishments. Students need to develop good sound skills in the foundations of English and Mathematics. Universities still like to see students who are well-qualified in the traditional subjects.

This college has always had a reputation for a traditional curriculum and I believe this should be continued. I shall therefore ask the candidates for their opinion of the new initiatives in teaching that we hear about all the time.

I also feel that the other members of the appointments board should pay attention to my opinions as I am the most senior teaching representative on the board.

Board Member IV

This board member's character and views may be devised by the student taking part in this exercise. Read through the other board members' descriptions and then write one to describe yourself.

Candidate I

I am the Vice-Principal of Welling College. I have held this post for the past three years. In that time I have seen an unfortunate decline in student numbers and an increasingly low morale amongst staff. I believe the reason for this decline has been because we have not kept pace with changes in curriculum development, changes that our local comprehensive school has certainly taken full advantage of. We have insisted on

offering traditional A levels when, frankly, the general trend now is to become more commercially linked.

Another reason for the college's decline is the very good parents' association at Welling Comprehensive. They have been able to expand their courses thanks to financial help from those parents. We have no such fund-raising organisation and I do not believe we are the sort of institution that could easily run one as parents tend not to get so involved in further education. I believe that the local education authority should recognise this and increase our budget. If I were to become principal I should seek much more student participation in decisions about the curriculum; for far too long we have neglected the rights of our students.

Candidate II

I am the Principal of a small London college. I am applying for this post as I would like to move away from the big city, and I would like the challenge of enhancing this college's reputation in the county. I feel that I am well-qualified to build up the college's standing in the community. I have been in a very similar position in my present post: I spent the first two years there gaining development grants from the council for an overseas contract to teach English to staff in a French company based in Oxford Street and for a contract with a local employment agency to teach its staff communication skills. I also started a scheme whereby interested parents could contribute their skills voluntarily as helpers to lecturers in some of the practical classes. It is my belief that a college needs a strong person in charge, someone who will increase its financial budget and also build up its reputation for upholding good solid educational methods. If parents can see that a college can guarantee their students a place in higher education, then they will surely make every effort to support that college.

Candidate III

This candidate's character and views may be devised by the student taking part. Read through the other candidates' descriptions and then write one to describe yourself.

7   Effective Meetings

INTRODUCTION

Business meetings can vary in their type, purpose, scope, size, content and style. They can range from the large, formal gathering where rules and procedures are closely defined and strictly followed, to the small, informal meeting between two or three people who have got together to discuss some common interest. Most day-to-day business meetings tend towards the informal type. Some form of control is obviously necessary, but the over-use of procedures and formality will often stifle – or at least restrict – free thought and discussion.

We are concerned here with the normal business meeting, whose effectiveness (or otherwise) can be measured in terms of the quality, clarity, economy and relevance of its discussion and result, and the speed with which questions are resolved and action taken. We are not so much concerned with formal gatherings where rules and procedures tend to carry a disproportionate importance, and where the opportunity to voice opinions, put forward motions, pass resolutions and vote on issues is an essential part of the proceedings.

As with other forms of communication, meetings will only be effective when the following procedures are observed:

— there has been proper preparation;
— the aim is clear and understood by everyone;
— the possible existence of barriers has been recognised and plans made to overcome them;
— content is relevant;
— communication takes place in an ordered manner;
— checks are made to see if the aim is being/has been achieved;
— those involved possess and use the necessary skills.

PREPARATION

There are two aspects to preparing for a meeting (see Figure 7.1): making the administrative arrangements, and preparing for the conduct

PREPARATION

- **Admin**
- **Information**
- **Purpose**   (chair)
- **Resources**   (chair)
- **Anticipate**   (chair)
- **Plan**   (chair)
- **Relevance**   (all)
- **Ordered**   (chair)
- **Monitored**   (chair)
- **Skills**   (all)

Figure   7.1

of the meeting itself. The administrative arrangements will cover such things as choosing the right people to attend and selecting a convenient date, time and place; sending out the convening instructions, particularly details on the aim of the meeting and its agenda and any background material that may be necessary; arranging for seating, place cards, stationery, secretarial support, telephones, refreshments, reception, etc. The extent to which these various arrangements are necessary will of course depend on the size, formality and complexity of the meeting.

Although all of these points carry some importance – particularly those concerned with circulating the aim and agenda – many of them are nothing like as essential to the conduct of an effective meeting as is sometimes thought. It is perfectly possible to conduct an effective meeting in *ad hoc* and even disagreeable physical circumstances, provided there has been adequate preparation for the conduct of the meeting itself!

Whoever is going to chair the meeting must obviously prepare him/herself for it – and if it is to be effective, so must each member. It is essential that the Chairman comes to the meeting with a very clear idea of the purpose of the meeting, his aim, and how he intends to achieve it. None of this implies a rigid, authoritarian approach – the plan must always be flexible and responsive to the particular characteristics of the meeting. There must, however, be some kind of plan. Just as one would not think of setting off on a journey without a clear idea of destination, route, methods of transport, obstacles, etc, so a Chairman should not convene a meeting without equally careful thought and planning. To achieve a successful plan the following points should be observed:

— Be quite clear as to the purpose of the meeting;
— Meetings can be called for various reasons, and the type of meeting will often influence its conduct.
— Decide on the main aim. This should be done as precisely as possible, and limits established. The aim should be capable of being expressed in such a way that it is perfectly understood by everyone present at the meeting; the goal to be reached by the meeting should be clearly defined and progress towards achieving that aim should be measured.
— The Chairman should also consider the resources he will have available, ie the knowledge and skills of the various members; how he can best use these resources.
— Try to anticipate any likely obstacles and difficulties; consider how they might be overcome.
— Develop a plan for getting the meeting from its starting point to its desired goal as effectively as possible, and make sure the discussion does not stray too far away from the relevant subject.
— Each member should be informed of and think about the purpose and aim of the meeting in advance. This will help to get a common understanding of the task established as quickly as possible.
— Anticipate the possible course of discussion.

— Gather information and references.
— Decide which topics or points should be raised and prepare a plan to have these views and opinions put across.
— Anticipate any reactions and objections, and plan to counter them.

Although not a conscious part of the preparation for any particular meeting, the acquisition and development of the skills needed for effective participation – whether as Chairman or member – is implicit in the overall process of 'preparation'.

CONDUCT AND STRATEGIES

The two most important requirements for effective meetings are that communication should take place in an ordered manner, and that content should be relevant. Too often it is assumed that both these are the responsibility of the Chairman, who achieves them by 'controlling' the meeting. There are obviously instances when such 'control' is necessary, but responsibility for orderly communication and relevance lies with every individual member. Both requirements can in fact be achieved without a Chairman at all – if every member adopts the self-discipline needed to achieve an effective meeting (see Figure 7.2). In some cases, control of the discussion can change hands during a meeting, resting at any point in time with the member who appears to be best qualified to deal with the particular phase the discussion has reached.

There is no instant recipe for the effective conduct of a meeting. However, some important ingredients do exist and should always be present. The aim of the meeting, for instance, must be clearly understood by all present. This aim may be defined by the Chairman, or evolved by discussion, but it must be understood and accepted by everyone present before the discussion goes any further. Its limits must be drawn clearly enough in everyone's mind for them to recognise at once when they are straying off the point. If the meeting is seeking an end product, then this too must be defined sufficiently clearly for everyone to recognise either its achievement, or the extent to which it has *not* been achieved.

It is also often helpful for the meeting to agree an outline plan for achieving its goal. For example, a complex subject can sometimes be broken down into stages. Identifying and agreeing these stages early in the meeting can help to control its progress and improve the relevance of the discussion.

CONDUCT

- Self - discipline
- Definition of aims
- Stages
- Contribution
- Progress
- Agreement

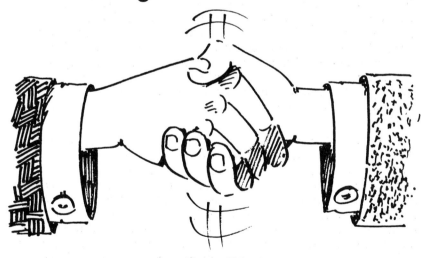

Figure 7.2

From time to time, progress towards the goal should be checked. This may be done by the Chairman, or by any other member of the meeting. The essential point is that there should be an opportunity for everyone to review how things are going, and to make any necessary adjustments. Everyone present must also have the opportunity to contribute his or her views. This may mean restraining some members, and encouraging others – often the most difficult task facing a Chairman, and one that requires great skills. At the end of the meeting, before members disband, its outcome and the way it has gone should be assessed. Agreement should also be reached on what action should be taken and what remains to be done.

FOLLOW-UP AND MINUTES

No meeting can be said to have been effective until any follow-up action agreed upon has been completed. Although it is important to circulate minutes as quickly as possible, details of what follow-up action is necessary should, as indicated above, be agreed before members disperse.

The writing of minutes requires considerable skill. The aim is to record the essentials without giving a blow-by-blow account of the meeting, yet not leaving out anything important. Unless the meeting wishes to have a particular point of view stated in full and its author identified, it is usually sufficient to record decisions in the form 'It was agreed that . . .'. Another useful tip is to include an 'Action By' column on the right hand margin of each page. The appointment or name of the person required to take action is entered in this column, opposite the item concerned. This makes it much easier to see who is required to do what, and allows progress on action taken to be checked. Apart from accuracy, the most important thing about minutes is that they should be circulated as soon as possible after the meeting, whether for approval or for executive action by the members.

EFFECTIVE AND INEFFECTIVE GROUPS (see Figure 7.3)

A Comparison

	Effective Group	Ineffective Group
Objectives	The aims and objectives of the group have been clearly formulated and are understood and accepted by all members.	The objectives are not clearly defined, let alone universally known and accepted. Often conflict arises because individuals have their own personal private aims, or in the absence of stated aims assume them.

EFFECTIVE AND INEFFECTIVE GROUPS

* Objectives
* Relevance
* Participation/ listening
* Atmosphere
* Criticism
* Conflict
* Feelings
* Decision-making
* Follow-up
* Leadership
* Group working

Figure 7.3

	Effective Group	Ineffective Group
Relevance of discussion	Much relevant discussion, with virtually everyone contributing.	Tends to be dominated by a few; matters discussed are often irrelevant.

	Effective Group	**Ineffective Group**
Participation and listening	Everyone is prepared to listen to each other and consider the points made. Members are not afraid to put forward their own views and ideas.	Members do not give each other a fair hearing; contributions are often irrelevant and made for effect. It is clear that some members are hesitant to state their views, fearing ridicule or condemnation by stronger members.
Atmosphere	Tends to be informal, relaxed, and shows that all members of the group are involved and interested.	Formal, tense, with undercurrents of antagonism. There is obvious indifference and boredom.
Criticism	Accepted as being a constructive element and welcomed.	Often destructive and made as a result of personal antipathies.
Handling of conflict	Disagreements are not suppressed, but are carefully examined, and attempts are made to resolve them. Dissenters are not dominated nor is there 'tyranny of the minority'.	Disagreements may either be completely suppressed or result in open conflict. Often a vote is taken, and while a small majority get their way, a large minority are dissatisfied. Sometimes a sub-group will be so aggressive that the majority give way to maintain peace and working order.
Expression of personal feelings	Members feel free to express their own feelings and attitudes towards the problem under discussion.	Personal feelings are often kept hidden under the surface.

	Effective Group	**Ineffective Group**
Decision making	Decisions are arrived at by consensus. The individual, however, is not afraid to disagree and is given fair consideration. Formal voting is seldom used and a simple majority is not considered a suitable basis for action.	There is no systematic discussion or consideration of everyone's views. Decisions are arrived at without overall agreement and often action is taken prematurely. Formal voting is frequently used, even when a small majority means that many disagree and remain resentful.
Follow-up action	When decisions and follow-up action are determined, everyone is fully aware of this, and jobs are allocated clearly and appropriately.	Neither decisions nor actions are clearly defined, and when tasks are handed out, there is always the possibility that they will not be fulfilled.
Leadership	The Chairman does not dominate nor are the members subservient to him. In fact the leadership role may shift according to the circumstances to the most appropriate person with the most knowledge and experience.	The leadership may be jealously guarded by the Chairman, whether he is weak or strong, capable or not. Alternatively, there may be a struggle for leadership in order to exert influence or achieve status.
Group working	The group is aware that to operate efficiently, it must frequently review what it is doing and maintain a self-conscious attitude towards the way it is working.	The group is not prepared to acknowledge or discuss its own deficiencies, at least not in the meeting proper.

LIMITING FACTORS

* Experience

* Knowledge

* Fear

* Behaviour

* Dominance

Figure 7.4

Limiting Factors (see Figure 7.4)

Many of the above points may seem obvious, but experience shows that this is not necessarily so. The question therefore is 'Why?'. There appear to be a number of possible explanations:

— people's experience of really effective groups is very limited, and there are no clear standards to go by;
— few people have knowledge of the factors that distinguish effective from ineffective groups;
— fear of conflict, hidden hostilities and underlying personal factors are difficult to overcome.

Yet another inhibiting factor in the success and effectiveness of a meeting is the misapprehension that the effectiveness of a group rests solely with the leader. In fact, research indicates that it is skilful membership behaviour which is the operative factor. The greatest danger of all is that the person with the loudest voice or strongest personality will become Chairman and totally dominate the meeting, so that those who have relevant knowledge and opinions are not heard.

TYPES AND SIZES OF MEETING

Purposes

It is difficult to lay down hard and fast rules for classifying meetings and discussions. Sometimes they are confined to one category but they may also take in several categories (see Figure 7.5). It is important, however, to be quite clear about the purpose of any meeting or discussion and a list of common reasons for calling a meeting is given below.

Giving Information:

— to hear a statement of policy;
— to receive instructions, or learn about new procedures;
— to brief a group of subordinates.

Note: opportunities may be given for questions and/or discussion.

Obtaining Information or Ideas:

— to hear subordinates' views on a problem;
— to find out what happened;
— to investigate a situation;
— to obtain information for a report.

Note: this type of meeting does not necessarily come to any decision, but usually involves discussion.

Progressing or Co-ordinating Activities:

— to discuss what action is needed;
— to co-ordinate the work of different sections or departments.

PURPOSES OF MEETING

* Give information
* Seek ideas
* Co-ordinate
* Release
* Involve
* Negotiate
* Resolve
* Policy
* Plan
* Decide
* Act

Figure   7.5

Airing Feelings or Grievances:

— to allow people to 'let off steam', for example.

Negotiating a Contract or Agreement:

— with Trade Unions or a contractor, for example.

Resolving a Problem:

— to clear up confusion;
— to overcome an obstacle to the implementation of a plan;
— to discover what the problem is;
— to investigate a technical difficulty.

Taking Non-executive Action:

— to get their support for a plan of action;
— to get their views and ideas;
— to develop their capabilities;
— to motivate them and get commitment.

Taking Executive Action:

— to get something done;
— to carry out a higher management plan.

  Note: information may move from one person outwards, from many persons inwards or be multi-directional (see Figure 7.6).

Formulating Policy:

— about the use of certain equipment, for example.

Preparing a Plan or Recommendations:

— to formulate proposals for senior management to consider, for example.

Reaching a Decision:

— how to apply a plan;
— what to do about something or someone.

Sizes (see Figure 7.7)

— *Two people* – impractical since biased or freakish decisions are likely. Each person can exercise a complete veto over the other.

— *Three people* – tendency for two members to unite against the third. The odd one out is likely to withdraw into him- or herself (stop being productive), or set up a damaging protest movement. Three-man meetings also lack the error-correcting characteristics of larger groups.

COMMUNICATION PATTERNS IN GROUPS

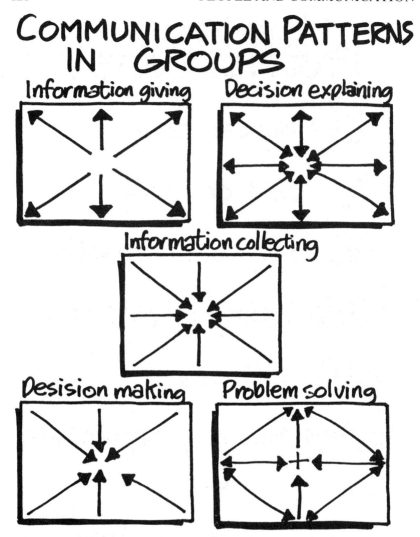

Figure   7.6

— *Four people* – sharp divergences tend to appear – three against one or two against two. Meetings of this size may have insufficient breadth of experience among members and be too lacking in variety and intellectual stimulus to produce good results.

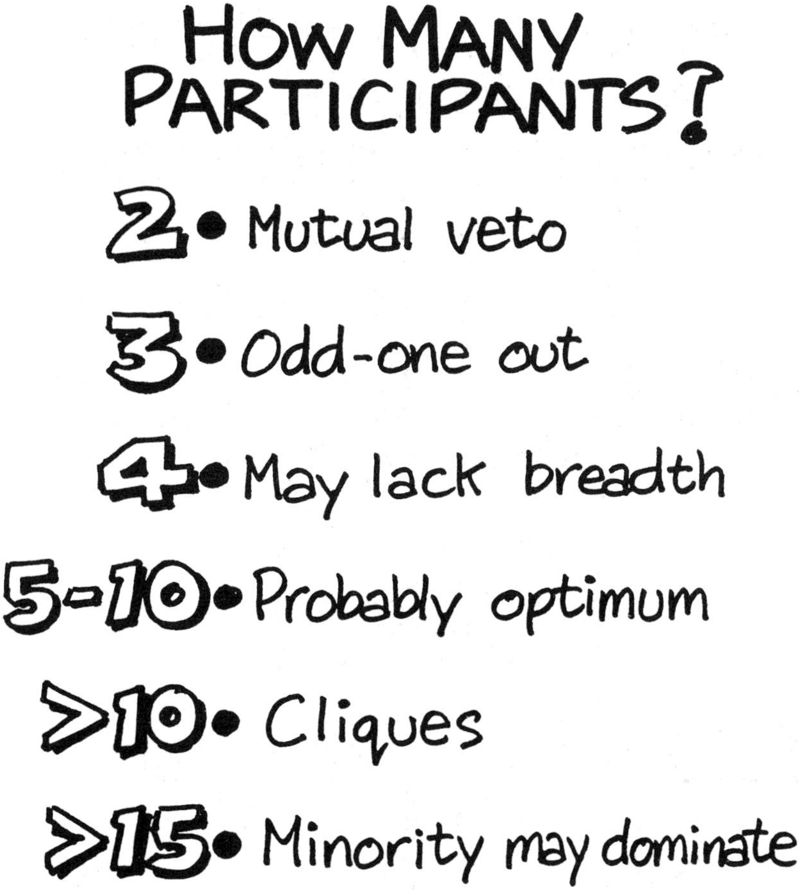

HOW MANY PARTICIPANTS?

2 • Mutual veto

3 • Odd-one out

4 • May lack breadth

5-10 • Probably optimum

>10 • Cliques

>15 • Minority may dominate

Figure   7.7

— *Five to ten* – people can talk nearly as much as they want to and are able to exert influence over each other. There is probably sufficient variety of talent and personality to treat problems imaginatively. Good conditions for interaction and therefore for group problem-solving.

— *Over ten* – as the group grows in numbers an increasing number of people are scared into silence. Intimate face-to-face contact becomes difficult and the group may split into cliques.

— *Over fifteen* – low participators stop talking to other members of the group and either stay silent or talk only to the few. Thus interaction – and creativity – freeze. Some large groups, however, can solve certain kinds of problem more effectively than similar smaller groups – eg where there is a correct and variable answer, say, the cheapest method of erecting a fence or building a cycle

REQUISITE SKILLS
* Formulation – definition
* Research
* Illustration
* Clarity
* Analysis
* Leading
* Summarising
* Deducing
* Responsive
* Stimulating
* Steering
* Constructive
* Reconciling
* Listening
* Observing
* Assessing

Figure   7.8

shed. In addition, the more people in the group the more chance there is that it contains an expert who knows the answer.

REQUISITE SKILLS

'Skill' is defined as 'the ability to do something'. In a meeting or discussion many different kinds of things have to be done to produce effective results (see Figure 7.8). For instance the aim needs to be stated; facts need to be elaborated; ideas need to be linked and related; conclusions have to be drawn. By virtue of their experience and personal characteristics, some people are better at doing some of these things than others. An effective meeting is one where these skills are recognised, and used to the benefit of all. The Chairman alone cannot be expected to be equally strong in all skills. Members must therefore use their own strengths to supplement those of the Chairman.

Here are some examples of the skills that need to be exercised by a competent Chairman and some of the techniques involved:

Formulating aims/ *Stating aims*	Defining the aim; re-wording statements; writing down aims.
Seeking information/ *Seeking opinions*	Asking for facts; searching out ideas; formulating relevant questions.
Giving information/ *Giving opinions*	Offering relevant information; putting forward ideas or opinions; giving examples to stimulate discussion.
Clarifying/ *Elaborating*	Clearing up confusions; interpreting ideas or suggestions; questioning meaning; asking for elaboration of a point; clarifying purpose.
Analysing	Breaking down ideas; deciding what is relevant or significant; identifying the ingredients of a problem.
Proposing	Making firm propositions about what should be done next; leading the discussion forward.
Summarising	Linking related ideas; re-wording suggestions; putting forward intermediate conclusions; summarising progress.

Deducing/ *Drawing conclusions*	Bringing discussion to an effective conclusion; sending up 'trial balloons'; making deductions from information given.

There are also other kinds of things that need to be done mainly concerned with helping people to work together:

Creating confidence/ *Creating security*	Putting people at ease; being warm and friendly; being responsive to people's contributions; showing regard for others.
Encouraging/ *Stimulating*	Encouraging participation; encouraging silent members' participation; helping people to use their skills; sparking off thought.
Steering	Suggesting ways in which progress might be made; re-directing the course of discussion; helping the meeting to adjust its methods of working.
Supporting	Being constructive; building and developing other people's ideas and contributions; preventing good ideas or useful facts from being lost; making your own view clear.
Reconciling	Exploring differences; emphasising similarities.
Listening	Really concentrating on what other people are saying; being less concerned with your own personal contribution; thinking, but not interrupting.
Observing	Watching what is happening and how people are reacting; noting pressures or tensions; monitoring progress towards the aim.
Reviewing/ *Assessing*	Assessing how far the aim is being achieved; identifying what is helping or hindering progress.

How Do You Rate as a Chairperson?

Read through the following points and tick as appropriate.

1 I vary my style according to the purpose of the meeting.

2 I know how to deal with 'hidden agenda' items – power struggles, jealousies, rivalries, etc – and so relieve the group's inner tensions.

3 I encourage people to bring their negative feelings out into the open by skilful questioning and careful listening.

4 I try not to let members quarrel over mere words and generalisations. When two people disagree I ask each one to specify the factor(s) they disagree with and give examples of what they mean.

5 Sometimes I deliberately reduce my own authority in meetings in order to create a freer atmosphere. I know three techniques for doing this.

6 If people wander from the problem-path I know how to call them back *with tact.*

7 I know the kind of seating arrangements which encourage interaction.

8 I help the committee to keep track of its progress by summarising the discussion from time to time and by keeping a record of promising ideas for future reference.

9 I don't overwork the committee, and give it adequate time to solve complex problems. If time is limited I shorten the agenda.

10 At the end of the meeting I summarise the ground covered, decisions made and any action to be taken and by whom.

8   Taking Sides

INTRODUCTION

Taking sides is a part of normal human activity, both verbal and non-verbal. Even non-verbal activities, such as football, call forth strong verbal support for one team and abuse for the other, but we are here concerned with those activities whose main content is verbal rather than physical.

We take sides in a discussion, a debate, an argument, a negotiation. Newspaper reporters and editors take sides in the emphasis they give to the virtues of one political party or political system, the government or the trades unions, the North or the South, the East or the West, and so on.

In this chapter, we concentrate on two aspects of verbally taking sides: negotiating, with the purpose of achieving a settlement satisfactory to both sides, and commenting, with the purpose of justifying one course of action or party, while vilifying another. We will take this latter aspect first.

SLANTED COMMENT

Emotive Words

Some newspapers (the extreme minority) do their best to report objectively, giving equal weight to both sides and leaving the readers to form their own conclusions. An example, taken from *The Guardian* of 19 June 1984, is shown in Figure 8.1. Re-write this article as you would imagine it would appear in a typical left-wing, or trade union newspaper report, then re-write it as a typical right-wing newspaper report.

Two expressions which occur frequently in newspaper reports are 'terrorist' and 'freedom fighter'. Can you think of other pairs of words which biased reporting might employ to describe a single event or person. Here are a few examples to start you off: diplomat/trickster; guerilla/murderer; party/junta; catholic/papist; social democrat/red; leader/gauleiter; gunman/patriot; businessman/robber; buxom/fat; brave/foolhardy; colourful/gaudy; decorative/pretentious; steadfast/obstinate; loyal/sycophantic, etc.

ł. counts of Scargill injury clash

Black day for picket battle violence

By Malcolm Pithers

The worst scenes of violence in the miners' dispute broke out at the Orgreave coking plant near Rotherham, Yorkshire, yesterday with cars being burned, stones, bricks and bottles being hurled, and policemen lashing out with truncheons.

The battle lasted for 10 hours of horrific clashes. At the end 93 had been arrested and 79 injured — 51 of them pickets and 28 police officers.

Among the injured was the miners' president, Mr Arthur Scargill who was detained in Rotherham Infirmary last night for observation.

His condition was not serious and hospital staff said he suffering from head, arm

Violence fails to shift Thatcher, page 2; Parliament, page 20

and leg injuries. He was taken to hospital amid conflicting versions of how his injuries were sustained.

Mr Scargill said he believed he was struck by a police shield from behind. The assistant chief constable of South Yorkshire, Mr Tony Clement, said he was standing only a few yards from the miners' president and saw him fall on a railway banking.

He said Mr Scargill struck himself accidentally against what looked like a railway sleeper.

Mr Clement said he could not speak for what may have happened earlier, but he saw Mr Scargill standing near two men. The miners' leader had

Mr Clement — "saw miners' leader slip"

slipped near some chain link fencing and fallen down backwards.

Mr Clement said that the miners' leader then struck the back of his head on what he, Mr Clements, thought was the sleeper.

He went across to talk to Mr Scargill and found him obviously concussed. He spoke to the men nearby and told them Mr Scargill needed help. They told him that two lads would look after him, but Mr Clement insisted that Mr Scargill needed professional help as soon as possible.

Another account of what happened came from a miner, Mr Stephen Hallow from Silverwood Colliery, who said that the police charged towards them.

He said he saw Mr Scargill on the floor cut of the corner of his eye. He said as far as he was concerned he had been given a " good leathering."

Police riot squads were used yesterday and several mounted police charges were made. Throughout the day missiles of every size and type were

hurled towards police lines.

At one point the police said that two petrol bombs had been thrown. But it seemed later that there had been canisters of bottles filled with diesel fuel.

In an attempt to cool the situation magistrates ordered all pubs within two miles of the plant to stay shut at lunchtime. The order was made at the request of the South Yorkshire Chief Constable, Mr Peter Wright. Police then toured pubs and off licences ordering them to close.

Miners began converging on the Orgreave plant at 3am yesterday. Some had travelled from Scotland, Wales, the North-east of England as well as Yorkshire.

At one stage they practically overwhelmed police units There were pitched battles inside the coking plant for the first time since picketing began, and the frustration on both sides spilled over into sickening scenes of miners being batoned and of police being attacked with bricks, slivers of glass as well as the containers of fuel.

Although the police lines eventually held, officers did react violently. Truncheons were drawn and used on individuals by snatch squads. The day produced unreal, pitiful scenes. Cars were rolled downhill towards policemen and ignited to make a flaming barricade.

At one point I heard a policeman yell at a photographer to take photographs of a hero. He was pointing to a mounted police officer whose arm was bleeding badly. An ambulanceman was holding the wound to stem the flow of blood.

. It was equally sickening to hear policemen clapping and cheering as a picket, bleeding heavily from a head wound, was helped into an ambulance. While this was happening police were being pelted with missiles.

At the height of the battle two men who run a local transport works a few hundred yards from the plant found miners battering down the doors of their works. They told Mr Ashton Whittingham and Neil Manning that the police had been filming them from his garage.

A diesel tank was then emptied and bottles and canisters filled. Vehicles inside were hauled out and used in the barricade.

Earlier in the day I had walked with miners converging on the plant near this garage. At that time there was a peaceful mood.

Later I returned to the same spot to find the barricade across the road. A few yards further on wooden stakes had been placed in lines to prevent any police horse charges.

The barrage of rocks, bricks and glass was kept up for hours. For most of this time policemen stood with riot shields to fend off the missiles. Charges were also made against the pickets with policemen lashing out with truncheons.

Mr Clement, who is in charge of the Orgreave operation, said later that it was a miracle no one had been killed. What people had witnessed could only be called a riot.

Figure   8.1   Excerpt from *The Guardian*, 19 June 1984

Now check *The Guardian* report of 26 June 1984 (see Figure 8.2): is it completely free of bias? Visit the nearest library and look in various newspapers to find opposing accounts of a given person or event; note down the different words used in these accounts. You can then compare your lists with those of fellow students. Learn to recognise emotive words and their emotive opposites, and ask yourself what effect an account would have on you if the other words of the pair had been used.

Fear is the legacy of temple siege

SINCE the assault on the Golden Temple, the Punjab has been virtually sealed off from the rest of India and the world. Guardian correspondent Ajoy Bose has travelled through the army-occupied province to bring out the first full reports on the troubled and angry mood of Punjabis, and their fears for the future.

THE FRAGILITY of the peace in the Punjab countryside becomes apparent even in casual conversation. Hindus and Sikhs express sharply contrasting viewpoints, indicating the deep-rooted polarisation that exists between the two communities.

Among Hindus, there is unanimous relief at the mili-

tary crackdown and the death of Sant Bhindranwale and his band of extremists who had terrorised them for three months. Those people inside the Golden Temple were murderers and they were out to murder Hindus specially. Thank God that Indiraji had finally the sense to send the army against them," said Hindu businessman in Chandigarh, the state capital of Punjab.

Sikhs on the other hand seem quite disoriented at the events of the past month. Their moods vary from anger and defiance to helplessness and fear, from grief and sorrow to a feeling of humiliation bristling with resentment.

"We will not forget and we will not forgive," said Sucha Singh, an elderly Sikh peasant, member of the local

council of a cluster of villages in Kapurthala district 60 mile south of Amritsar.

The peasant leader is angry about a lot of things. Like most other members of his community, he sees the army assault on the Golden Temple as the supreme insult to his faith. He is angry with the combing operations

ence of the army underlines the tension that exists. Soldiers carrying sten guns stop and search all vehicles, including bullock carts and tractors, every few miles along the highways. Army trucks fitted with machine-guns rumble down city streets carrying soldiers with their rifles pointed suspiciously at every passer-by.

A few made the mistake of fleeing when soldiers asked them to identify themselves. Others paid with their lives for their curiosity and were shot down as suspected snipers while they sneaked upon roof tops to see the extent of damage to the Golden Temple.

The most unfortunate incident of this sort happened two days after the army had entered the temple, when troops shot dead 10 sevadars

(social workers) of the famous Sikh saint, Baba Kharak Singh, in a raid in the city.

In Ropar district, a few miles from Chandigarh, angry Sikh villagers living near the Bhakra canal cut the water supply link to the neighbouring Hindu dominated state of Haryana shortly after the army entered the temple.

The Government imposed a punitive fine of 10 million rupees on the 50-odd villages around the canal, but villagers in the area are openly defiant and vow that they will not pay.

The anger and defiance of the Sikh peasantry is tempered by a sense of helplessness and fear at the superior firepower and discipline of the troops patrolling the highways.

Pilgrims flock to Amritsar, page 7

that the army and paramilitary forces have carried out in his village and the consequent arrest of many of his friends and relatives. But Sucha Singh is also disgusted with the Akali Dal leadership for leading the Sikhs to their present sorrows.

The overwhelming pres-

Figure 8.2 Excerpt from *The Guardian*, 26 June 1984

Honest and Dishonest Use of Emotion

Recognising that there are these pairs of emotive words does not mean condemning all emotional use of language. Emotion moves us to action; reason on the other hand only causes us to search for contrary reasons if a case is one which, emotionally, we cannot support. An appeal on behalf of starving children, or mistreated prisoners, for instance, is inevitably directed at the emotions, but may none-the-less be honest. Someone who incites a crowd to string up a suspect, however, or gets up a petition to stop a new road being built on the grounds that it will be unsafe for children, while really thinking only of the effect on himself or on the value of his house, is using emotion dishonestly. Such things occur every day, in business as well as private life. Look out for examples if you want to learn more about unbiased communication.

False Argument

A device frequently used in argument, is to say event b happened after event a, therefore b was caused by a (*post hoc, ergo propter hoc*). In the Middle Ages witches were burnt at the stake on this kind of false reasoning, and today many reputations are lost and businesses damaged in the same way.

Another variant of the false argument is false analogy: money flows through a business as blood flows through the body, therefore without money, business is impossible; the body must do as the head commands, therefore we must all obey the commands of our (political or other) 'leader'. Again, look out for examples of this kind of reasoning in your discussions and in your reading.

NEGOTIATION

Negotiators have to be careful in looking for arguments to support their position, not to fall into any of the verbal traps just discussed. Politicians and persuaders of all types use them as a matter of course, and rely on the emotion of the moment to save them from exposure. In contrast, a negotiator who uses any of these tricks will almost certainly be exposed, and once exposed will have difficulty in ever recovering his credibility.

Negotiation is an art. No-one can become a good negotiator merely by following a set of rules, firstly because all personalities are different and have to be differently used to get the best effect in negotiation, and secondly because no set of negotiations is quite like another – the personalities, issues and circumstances are always slightly different. So negotiation is an art which has to be studied and is not a routine that can be learnt. It can only really be successfully developed by experience; however, clarification of the dynamics of negotiation can help us develop our skills (see Figure 8.3).

Figure   8.3

Collecting the Information

First of all get the facts straight – and make sure you have all of them
– agreements, works rules, safety rules, etc. If the issue in dispute is a
grievance then get information on the following:

— the people involved;
— their job classification, shifts and rates;
— the time and place of the grievance and the departments involved;
— what has been violated, ie the agreement, custom and practice, or
  law.

If the dispute is a wage claim, collect all the relevant information
including the type of facts and arguments likely to be used by the other
side and include the following:

— movements in the cost of living and deficiencies in the price
  index;
— comparisons with other workers – their earnings and rates and
  whether the increases were granted through Wages Councils or
  arbitration; the adequacy of existing rates and earnings;
— movements in productivity (especially productivity per man hour),
  and the part played by the workers and by additional investment;
— changes in the profit position of the company;
— the likely effects of resultant price increase on the company's
  prospects and profits.

Preparing Your Case

Make sure the facts are relevant to the problem. Do not use hearsay
and remember that opinions do not constitute facts in most cases, eg if
someone says that a supervisor is picking on someone, define the
incidences referred to, find out how often they occur and get specific
instances. Before formal negotiation takes place, decide what you hope
to gain and what you are willing to concede. Remember that what you
hope to gain is not always the same as what you may be asked for as a
negotiator. Ensure that the demands and suggestions are within
reasonable limits. Try also to anticipate probable alternative suggestions
that the other side may put forward.

Plan your presentation. Negotiations only too often become unnecessarily complicated because either the management or the unions have
prepared their cases with insufficient care. Select your strongest points
and decide when to use them, discarding your weak ones. Do not
introduce your arguments in a haphazard way – the whole presentation
should be logical and so careful pre-planning is essential.

You should also try to anticipate the arguments that may be put by the other side. Use your imagination if you have to describe situations of which you have not personally had experience, eg the possible effect of wage increases on the fortunes of a company or the effects of a rise in the cost of living on living standards. In doing this you should use reliable facts and not just guess at them.

Planning the Strategy

The use of a strategy will help you win your case. Strategy must be planned in advance and in this *timing* is important. Bargain when the other side is at its weakest, for instance. The most favourable times will of course differ according to the company, the industry and the economy, eg a trade union should not plan on being tough when there is a high degree of unemployment nor an employer when there is a scarcity of good labour. Use sensible bargaining methods and try to decide on an 'acceptable' settlement well in advance, for there is always a difference between what is demanded and the final negotiated settlement.

Decide in advance on the negotiating method which best suits your personality. Are you naturally forthright, tough or conciliatory? Should you allow your natural manner full rein or adapt it to the occasion and to the people you will meet on the other side of the negotiating table? To help you decide on a negotiating style, try to find out how the other side feels about the issues.

You should also think out the consequences of various types of approach and settlement. Do not try to 'pull a fast one'. Your case should be good enough to stand on its own merits. Deception is a poor weapon and while you may gain a temporary advantage a false case may result ... a wall of suspicion when next the two parties meet.

The Negotiating Table

— Step 1 – settle all the matters on which agreement can be reached so that you do not waste time and temper on unnecessary details. Some proposals may only need slight modification so the first efforts in bargaining are often merely exploratory.

— Step 2 – go through all the proposals; listen carefully and take notes of how the other side feels about them. Try to judge the ones on which they seem to feel most strongly as well as those on which there is obvious disagreement.

— Step 3 – decide on your opening tactic carefully. Should you use a cautious start and present only part of the case or put it all in one statement? As a general rule you should, as far as is possible, keep something up your sleeve. There is no need at the outset to tell all that is known about the case; a few salient facts will often suffice.

Note on adjournments – you should always adjourn to consider any new proposals or counter proposals. Never do your thinking aloud in front of the other side, and only renew discussion when you have carefully worked out a revised plan. If, however, you have already anticipated the new move, you can carry on with the negotiation without interruption.

Try not to get bogged down in prolonged argument over one or two minor items at the beginning of bargaining. Find out where the disagreement lies, how serious it is, and then pass on to the next point. Remember the successful bargainer is also a good listener. If either side wants only to talk and not to listen then no real bargaining can take place and there will be no basis for agreement. The art of listening and registering what is being said across the table as well as remembering the context in which key words and phrases have been employed, can mean the difference between success and failure. By doing this the bargainer can provide for snap decisions with a calculated evaluation of the intent of the other party and explore flaws in their argument.

It is important that members of the negotiation team rigidly observe the rule that they do not contradict one another during the negotiation and indeed do not speak unless asked to do so by the leader of their negotiating team. Instead make a written or whispered request for an adjournment. Do not be afraid to adjourn, it is not a sign of weakness.

Be brief and to the point. Do not just talk for the sake of talking – most negotiations are about practical matters. A business-like appr ach invariably ensures a quick response from the other side. Use plain language when putting a case or replying to one; this will keep the negotiation on the rails and prevent you from talking in circles.

Do not be unnecessarily tough unless you feel it is justified. In any case do not confuse toughness with noisiness. In fact as far as possible try to keep all hot-heads off the negotiation team. Lung power and bad temper are no substitute for a good case, well presented. Both sides should show the courtesy to the other that they expect themselves. This applies not only to the manner of speech but to matters of punctuality and general bearing as well. Throughout the negotiations, look for any change in the other side's attitude during the negotiations and be ready to alter your own to deal with them.

Ask yourself if you are making it easy for the other side to make concessions or at least to save face. Be flexible and firm. The most fair and carefully presented case may not succeed in spite of its fairness and logic. This may be because the other party remains unconvinced or is just plain stubborn. This kind of situation can be surmounted in one of two ways: *persuasion* or *compromise*. After the less contentious or disputable proposals have been settled, those which are left are likely to require the most negotiating skill. You must decide on your priorities at this stage and know which proposals are important and which are not. You must then be ready to re-word some of the proposals where necessary. Too many negotiators are rigid and inflexible in this matter and are either unwilling or unable to modify or amend proposals – they may do this because they have left themselves too little room in which to bargain, or because they have not prepared the case with enough care.

Throughout the negotiations, try not to confuse stubborness with firmness. You should decide well in advance the minimum settlements you are willing to accept. It is often those who are most rigid and inflexible who after bitter opening argument end up discussing counter proposals after abandoning their own ideas. This is usually because the other side has been able to put forward counter proposals which are less complicated.

The wise bargainer keeps on bargaining as long as the other party continues to do so in good faith, and there appears to be a chance of a settlement. But you should not concede anything simply in order to get a settlement. There is always a reasonable point beyond which you should not be prepared to bargain and you must learn to recognise this.

After the Negotiation

Always make some attempt to record the results. In order to be able to do this with confidence you must ensure throughout the bargaining that whenever a decision is made both sides are clear what it is and really do agree to it. Industrial relations is littered with examples of meetings where each side has left the negotiating table with a different impression of the result. Some of this can be considered to be deliberate but some is the result of genuine misapprehension.

At the close of negotiation the chances of further trouble are always considerably reduced if you make quite sure, at the time when the agreement is finalised, of all the details. If the last piece of business consists of a recapitulation of all the points the meeting has agreed to then few people will risk charges of breaches of faith by going back on them later. On the other hand an unstructured meeting where lots of things are said and none are recorded can lead to confusion.

Records of meetings can either be held separately by each side or, in the case of productivity bargains, for example, where there must be joint settlements, held jointly so that as few issues as possible are left only vaguely understood. Finally, make sure that both sides keep their word once an agreement is reached. Follow up the particular issues discussed a few weeks later to see that the terms of the settlement are being acted upon.

EXERCISE

It is June, the month of the annual wage negotiations in your firm, Vision Graphics. There are two main groups of employees: administrative staff (25) and technical staff (110). Administrative staff belong to the Union of Office and Allied Workers (UOAW). The UOAW is a small union with very little power to negotiate for its members. Its members are currently paid on a salary range of £4,000–£8,000. Last year they had an increase of 5%. Technical staff belong to the Union of Technical, Computing and Mechanical Operatives (UTCMO). This union has been expanding over the past five years and now has quite a powerful voice. Its members are currently paid on a salary range of £5,000–£11,000. Last year they had an increase of 5.9%.

Pay negotiations usually take place between a management team consisting of the Managing Director, Company Accountant and Personnel Manager, and a joint union team consisting of the Shop Stewards' Committee from both unions. However, this union team does not always manage to agree on a bargaining strategy before negotiations begin.

The management team base their wage negotiations on the following:

— keeping wages below the inflation rate (over the past twelve months it has stood at 5%);
— wages offered to comparable workers in similar industries;
— the end-of-year financial figures of the company.

All of the above figures are also available to union negotiators.

The union teams base their wage negotiations on the following:

Administrative Union

— keeping abreast of the inflation rate;
— seeking to raise their pay more in line with the technical staff.

Technical Union

— keeping abreast of the inflation rate;
— seeking to raise their pay level in line with their competitor company, Graphlinks Ltd (where salaries are between £5,500 and £12,500);

— the administrative staff use the same canteen as management, but the technical staff have their own. The technical staff therefore feel they are discriminated against, especially as they are often served chips, whereas in the other canteen more 'healthy' food is offered;

— some women in the UOAW have put in a plea for the last two years for a crèche to be made available for the use of their children. Their union may decide to push this demand further this year;

— both unions also want a shorter working week of 38 hours.

Recent Wage Settlements in Comparable Industries

Firm	Month settled	%	New salary scale Administrative staff	New salary scale Technical staff
Comptec Ltd	May	6	£4,600 – £8,700	£5,800 – £12,250
Graphlinks Ltd	March	5.4	£4,500 – £8,500	£5,500 – £12,500
Systems Go	Feb	5	£4,300 – £8,000	£5,300 – £11,000

Graphlinks Ltd is the most comparable to Vision Graphics in terms of location, size and production line. Comptec has had a great deal of government money invested in its initial growth stages which makes it a rather unusual company.

Pay increases over the past five years:

Vision Graphics	54%
Comptec Ltd	66%
Graphlinks Ltd	59%
Systems Go	51%

The weekly working hours for the past five years:

	1986	1985	1984	1983	1982
Vision Graphics	39½	39½	40	40	40
Comptec Ltd	38½	39	39½	40	40
Graphlinks Ltd	38	39	39½	40	40
Systems Go	39	39½	39½	39½	40

Analysis

In the light of the information gathered by the management team, the personnel director has to do four things:

— assess the case the union is likely to make;
— estimate the initial claim arising from that case and what the union may be prepared to settle for;
— set out the case the company should make in reply to the union claim;
— recommend the negotiating strategy to be used by the company.

Exercise

Working in groups, prepare either the union case or the management case. Now, using the cases prepared, role-play the negotiations.